P9-CBI-459

DATE DUE

76480
Truth and life

St. Procopius College Library
Maple Ave. and College Rd.
Lisle, Illinois

TRUTH AND LIFE

TRUTH AND LIFE

An Outline of Modern Theology

DONAL FLANAGAN
ENDA MCDONAGH
KEVIN MCNAMARA
DENIS O'CALLAGHAN

THE BRUCE PUBLISHING COMPANY

MILWAUKEE

St. Procopius College Library
Lisle, Illinois 60532

First American Edition 1969

2·30·2
T 77

© Donal Flanagan, Enda McDonagh
   Kevin McNamara, Denis O'Callaghan, 1968

Nihil obstat: Eduardus Gallen
              Censor Theol. Deput.

Imprimi potest: +Joannes Carolus,
               Archiep. Dublinen.
               Hiberniae Primas

             Dublini Die 10ª Augusti, 1968

Library of Congress Catalog Card Number: 69-12674

Printed and bound in the Republic of Ireland
by Cahill and Co. Limited, Dublin

76480

CONTENTS

..

INTRODUCTION

In seeking to translate the teaching of Vatican II and its theological foundations into the daily living of the Church, one of the most important tasks is to provide for the theological needs of the pastoral clergy. However much emphasis may now be placed on the role of bishops or laity, the religious understanding of most Christians depends today and for the immediate future on the priests in parishes and schools. Theologically and sociologically, given their professional training and official commitment, priests constitute an obvious centre in deepening and renewing, perhaps even revolutionizing, the Christian's grasp of the word of God. If priests lack this understanding themselves, the Christian community, local and universal, will have great difficulty in achieving it.

With this need uppermost in their minds the four contributors to this book set about devising a programme for priests in pastoral work. The programme aimed at giving the priests a survey of some of the main growth-points in theology and at stimulating and enabling them to carry on further reading and discussion from there. A useful extension of the service to the fifteen hundred or so priests who attended the course in Ireland and England would be, it was agreed, the publication of the actual lectures given. For this immediate purpose this book is intended.

It would be foolish to pretend that the lecturers did not envisage a wider public for the book than the priests who attended the original course. It is hoped that the book will be of help to other priests as well as to brothers, sisters and laypeople interested in theology. To enable the reader to get the best out of the book and to avoid raising false hopes, it is necessary to describe its origin and scope in more detail.

The first requirement of the good teacher is to start from where the learner is. And while no teacher can ever gauge exactly the mind of his pupil, still less the minds of fifteen hundred, the lecturers were conscious of the need not to presume too much reading by the priests of what is unfortunately known as the 'New Theology' and still more not to confuse them with fashionable, but to them strange and frequently unnecessary jargon. This should have the advantage of making the material accessible to others, also unfamiliar with much recent theological writing.

In selecting topics for discussion, preference was given not to the most controversial issues but to key-issues, that is to issues which were central to the Christian message as a whole. This quickly became an attempt to give some kind of rounded picture of the message in a way that will be outlined later.

At this stage what was in many ways to be the most distinctive feature of the course emerged. It was decided to present the course in units of two lectures. The first of these would be a dogmatic or doctrinal presentation of some basic aspect of the Gospel, the second would be a presentation of its implications for Christian living. In this way the word of God in its meaning and its demand would retain its unity and the harmful separation of dogmatic and moral theology would be overcome. At least in intention this was one of the most important aspects of the whole course.

The methodology of the lectures was as varied as the lecturers. One preferred a very comprehensive outline of his topic. Another preferred to develop a couple of points more intensively. The lecturers did not always agree on points, although the disagreement was naturally more in evidence on the platform, where questions deliberately exposed it, than it could be in a book on related but not identical topics. No attempt was made, of course, to suppress such disagreement and there has been no attempt to edit this book into a smooth party-line. The geographical collocation of the lecturers (they are all professors at St Patrick's

College, Maynooth) does not, we hope, rule out differences of approach and even conclusion. Yet, apart from the basic aims of educating and stimulating, the lectures reveal one common methodological factor. They are not surveys of other, no doubt worthier, people's opinions but the present personal understanding of the speakers themselves. The theologian, however limited he may consider himself, can never be a mere purveyor of the opinions of others, however gifted he may consider them. A theology that is not the product of his own reflection (using all the resources available within and without him) is not theology at all and of little value to listener or reader.

The strong Christological orientation of the course is soon apparent to the reader. As God's way and Word to man, Christ was and is also man's way and Word to God. In analysing this God-man dialogue in its origin and completion certain key-points selected themselves and the final plan seemed obvious to the lecturers. Beginning with revelation as God's word to man, the moral life as man's response to God formed with it a clear-cut unit. This word of God was his Son who became a word of redemption and reconciliation in the face of man's sinfulness. Incarnation and Redemption with sin and repentance were a natural second unit.

God's word to man was always a community-word. The theology of the Church develops this and is matched by the community-nature of man's response in the virtues of charity and justice. It is the *person*-in-community that the word ultimately transforms as the doctrine of grace elaborates. The personal response issues as faith, within which the Christian must live freely and form his conscience-judgements.

The effective word of God is a present reality and we see it visibly at work above all in the liturgy of the Eucharist. To these God-given signs corresponds the witness of particular human vocations, of which very particular and complementary instances are the vocations of marriage and celibacy.

Christ, Truth and Life, has not only present but future relevance; Christianity's eschatological dimension rounds off the doctrinal discussion and provides the basis for an examination of the virtue characteristic of the Christian's in-between existence, the virtue of hope.

The programme attempted here did not rely exclusively on the lectures given. In fact an attempt was made, with varying degrees of success, to limit each individual lecture to thirty minutes. The audience would then discuss among themselves in groups of eight to twelve the points of the lecture. This happened after the dogmatic and moral lecture in each unit. Then the chairmen of the different groups put the groups' questions or comments to the two lecturers involved. After the final session on the last evening of the three-day course, questions were invited from the floor to the panel of four lecturers together. With all this went a great deal of informal discussion at meals and so on. It is only in such an atmosphere and structure designed for give and take, that the original aims of the programme could be attempted. No book can substitute for the living understanding which can be achieved in such conditions.

Such a course, however successful, can only be a beginning. There must be a follow-through, especially in work by the priests themselves. The lecturers had the satisfaction of seeing such a follow-through organized after the first complete course. The Archbishop of Tuam, who had given the course its first home in May 1966, adopted a plan for further study by the priests to replace the old-style conferences. This plan, which operated through study-groups in the diocese, provided the priests with the stimulus and the structure they needed and prepared them for a further three-day conference in May 1967, devoted to the renewal of biblical studies. Similar group-study by the priests exists in many dioceses in Ireland today. It would be some satisfaction to feel that this book might contribute further to such study, not only among priests and not only in Ireland.

It would be discourteous of the lecturers not to express

once again their appreciation of the bishops who invited them and of the priests who received them so warmly, listened so carefully and not seldom disconcerted them by their questions. Through lecturing to learning was frequently the case in the exchanges which took place between the platform and the floor. Although it is hoped that the lecturers were not the only ones to return home wiser men, they would like to express their gratitude for that too.

Revelation:
God speaks to man

KEVIN McNAMARA

In the first chapter of the Dogmatic Constitution *Dei Verbum* the Second Vatican Council has given us an excellent *exposé* of the nature of divine revelation and of the historical process by which it was accomplished. This is the first methodical treatment of the subject in an official document of the Church's teaching authority. Vatican I touched upon it in its Constitution on the Catholic faith, but was concerned mainly with defining the relation between natural and supernatural revelation, and with affirming the role of the Church as authoritative interpreter of divinely-revealed truth. It is in this limited, apologetic perspective that revelation has been discussed in our modern theological manuals. The aim has been to prove that supernatural revelation is possible, can be recognized, and is in some sense necessary for mankind; and, with this established, to show the credibility of the Christian-Catholic faith as a religion divinely revealed. This approach has not been supplemented by any formal theological study of revelation itself. As a result our understanding of the new life with God to which faith introduces us has not been all it should be. For revelation is fundamental to the Christian life, being the act by which it is initiated, supported and continually renewed.

It is a surprising fact that we have had to wait until our

I

own day for a theological treatise setting out and analysing
the meaning of revelation. How has so basic a Christian
reality eluded for so long the attention of the Church's
teachers and theologians? No doubt the answer lies precisely
in revelation's fundamental role: from the beginning it was
accepted without question, and was assumed in the discussion of other topics which for various reasons came to the
forefront of the Church's consciousness. As commonly
happens in the development of a science, only when con-
siderable progress had been made in the effort of theology
to penetrate the faith, was it possible to grasp clearly the
fundamental importance of revelation and to appreciate
the need of a formal study of it. Not that the Church had
acquired no understanding of revelation in past times: she
understood and taught much about it, but as a subject
touched upon incidentally and implicitly, or as a reality that
was simply part of her life. Systematic study of it did not
come until the great modern onslaught on belief and on the
whole concept of the supernatural finally made it clear that
a thorough examination of the meaning of revelation was
called for.[1]

The Living God of Revelation

What then does revelation mean? A preliminary answer
to this question may be stated as follows: revelation is God
making himself known to man. This statement immediately
calls attention to the divine activity by which the message
is communicated, thereby helping to correct the recent one-
sided emphasis on the message itself which has tended to
isolate what was communicated from him who communicated it. We have tended to think of revelation mainly in
terms of doctrine, of truth communicated by God to man.
This has had unfortunate results, for it is impossible to understand the true significance and content of the message apart
from a study of the actual historical process by which God

---

[1]Cf. Gabriel Moran, *Theology of Revelation*, New York 1966, 22-3.

has chosen to communicate it. For what is most important in God's revelation to man is not any doctrine, even a doctrine about God, but God himself, who in revelation makes an entry into human history and confronts man as a living, acting God who wishes to enter into a personal relationship with him.

In revelation God does not simply give man a book in which to read about him. Knowledge imparted in this way would indeed be true, but indirect, impersonal and abstract. By intervening – one might even say intruding – in the events of human life, however, God imprints upon man's consciousness a powerful and unforgettable impression of himself. For the manner of God's disclosure of himself reveals him unmistakably as the Lord of history, as controlling and directing by his unlimited power the course of events that determine the destiny of individuals and peoples. At the same time God shows his dominion over the forces of nature, for his intervention is often miraculous, indicating absolute mastery of the laws which govern the universe. The God who works mighty wonders in the interests of his chosen people is evidently also the author of nature, the one who has created all things out of nothing and established the order which we find in them. For only he who had created the universe could hold sway over it and dispose of it in this sovereign manner. Thus, for the Israelites, dominated as they were by the consciousness of God's plan for his people and the experience of God's intervention in that people's history, creation appeared in an unmistakably religious light. The sea, the sky, the earth, the heavenly bodies, the various forces of nature all spoke to them eloquently of Yahweh, the Lord, of him who had taken the Israelites under his care and by his mighty acts led them out of Egypt, making them his own people for evermore. There was no hiatus, therefore, in the Israelites' conception of God: the God of nature and the God of salvation-history were one and the same. And this one God was a living God, for such he had unmistakably revealed himself. He was, in modern terms, a personal being, conscious, alert, watchful, ready to act, free from all constraint, demanding a return of love for love, dealing out rewards and punishments. 'Through the patriarchs, and after them through Moses and the prophets', we read in the Constitution *Dei Verbum*, 'he taught this nation to acknowledge himself as the one living and true God, provident Father and just Judge . . .'[2]

This is the heart of the message conveyed in God's revelation to his people, and it can only be appreciated by considering carefully the actual historical process by which God makes himself known. At first sight many may feel that the notion of a living, acting, personal God is quite commonplace, and no doubt it tells us nothing that we have not known already. But that is not to say that it may be taken for granted, or that we have not to remind ourselves of it continually, or try to acquire a firmer grasp of it and make it a more powerful force in our lives.

It is interesting, for example, to contrast it with the understanding of God achieved by the philosophers of ancient Greece. For them, at their best, God is the first cause, or unmoved mover, or supreme, self-existent good. In these abstract categories God remains remote. He does not concern the individual very closely. Who knows if he is a personal being or, if he is, what that might mean in one so completely transcending human experience? In his dealings with the world, has he a care only for the system in general, so that it is a matter of indifference to him how the individual fares, or even behaves, as long as the physical laws of the universe hold sway and the moral instinct which he has implanted in mankind ensures a certain minimum degree of reason and harmony in society? What is his attitude to me, personally? Does it concern him that I am lonely and frightened in this great, mysterious and often cruel universe? If I call upon him, will he answer? How can I have any con-

[2]*Dei Verbum*, art. 3.

fidence that he will, when I have called upon him so often before to no purpose? Has he *ever* answered a call from across that great abyss which separates him from mankind? Men have claimed that he has, but who can tell if they are not deceived? And if he should answer, what would he have to say? Would he speak a word of comfort and promise, holding out a hope of fulfilment, happiness and peace, perhaps even in some close relationship with himself? Or would his word be one of condemnation, pointing to my sins and abandoning me for ever to my own guilt?

These are some of the questions, so vital to man, that the Greek conception of God, for all its sublimity, leaves unanswered. If then we do find an answer in the biblical revelation, this is evidently something to be accepted, not as a matter of course, but with reverence and gratitude. Our own times bear this out, when many who seek a religious answer to life can feel no assurance that God is a personal being. They are unable to affirm any more than that he is their 'ultimate concern' or 'the ground of their being'. It may safely be said that such an approach to God, abstract and impersonal though it is, proves useful to some of our contemporaries who, because of defective presentation or some lack of insight, have not understood, or at any rate cannot accept, the Christian conception of God. Through their own limited approach they are led to go out of and beyond themselves and seek their fulfilment in the service of a noble ideal. In this way they may ultimately find salvation. Nevertheless, this does not give to such abstract and implicit notions of God anything more than the status of a *praeparatio evangelica*. They can never be accepted as a substitute for God as presented in the Bible, for the living, personal God of revelation.

To depersonalize God in this way is indeed a recurring temptation, and it would be naive to suppose that the widespread modern aversion to a personal God is due solely to a failure of understanding and not at all to moral factors Nor is it only modern secular man that is exposed to this temptation: even the traditional Christian theist must be on his guard lest the exacting demands of the personal God of the Bible lead him to replace this God with some abstraction. 'This should be carefully considered:' writes Cardinal Newman, 'we are apt to act towards God and the things of God as towards a mere system, a law, a name, a religion, a principle, not as against a Person, a living, watchful, present, prompt, and powerful Eye and Arm.'[3] The warning is repeated in our own day by C. S. Lewis who, with his usual verve, lays bare an attitude which often underlies pantheism, into which all merely abstract ideas of God are constantly in danger of merging:

> Men are reluctant to pass over from the notion of an abstract and negative deity to the living God. I do not wonder. Here lies the deepest tap-root of pantheism and of the objection to traditional imagery. It was hated not, at bottom, because it pictured him as man but because it pictured him as king, or even as warrior. The pantheist's God does nothing, demands nothing. He is there if you wish for him, like a book on a shelf. He will not pursue you. There is no danger that at any time heaven and earth should flee away at his glance .... An 'impersonal God' – well and good. A subjective God of beauty, truth and goodness, inside our own heads – better still. A formless life-force surging through us, a vast power which we can tap – best of all. But God himself, alive, pulling at the other end of the cord, perhaps approaching at an infinite speed, the hunter, king, husband – that is quite another matter.[4]

Revelation as God's Word

Let us now turn to the biblical story of revelation, which alone can safeguard us against thinking of God as an impersonal something. Fundamentally, what we find in the Bible is the story of God's call to man offering him personal

---

[3]*Parochial and Plain Sermons*, IV, London 1874, 31.
[4]C. S. Lewis, *Miracles*, London 1947, 113-4.

communion with himself. As a message from one person to another this call is appropriately designated 'God's word'. For a word is the privileged mode of communication between spiritual beings, an intelligible message communicating one's thought, emotion, or purpose. Thus we read in the Bible of God's word 'coming' to the prophets: God is using them to express and convey to his people the plan he has for them. The same is true of the mission of Moses to the captive Israelites: God's word has first called him, and he is now conveying that word to his brethren, and also to Pharaoh, to the former a word of salvation and hope, to the latter a word of stern command. In the light of this, one fact about God's word stands out clearly: it is not simply, or even primarily, a means of conveying to man a lesson or instruction; it is something much more personal and dynamic. By his word God is disclosing his plan for man and taking steps to put it into effect. His word, then, is his will, his eternal thought and purpose, now revealed.

As his will, God's word is identical with himself. Clearly, then, no human word can adequately express it. That is why God expresses himself to man in a whole series of human words, and not only in words but also in actions, gestures, symbols, institutions and indeed in the whole course of his people's history. The story of revelation is therefore the story of Israel and of God's dealings with it from the time of Abraham to the coming of Christ. Only through this vast and complex pattern of events, punctuated by explici divine messages interpreting and directing it, could God' word be effectively brought home to Israel.

Revelatory Acts and Words

Despite this complexity in modes of expression, God' word may nevertheless be said to appear in two primary forms, viz. deeds and (human) words. The Constitution on Divine Revelation highlights the two forms and describes their mutually complementary roles: 'This plan of revelation is realized by deeds and words having an inner unity: the

deeds wrought by God in the history of salvation manifest
and confirm the teaching and realities signified by the words,
while the words proclaim the deeds and clarify the mystery
contained in them.'[5]

Of the two, the deeds are the more striking. In them
God shows his dominion over man's destiny and the forces
of nature, acting powerfully to save his people and give
them victory and prosperity. The supreme example of God's
mighty deeds for Israel is of course the Exodus. This event,
by which the Israelites were led out from the slavery of
Egypt and brought to Mount Horeb to be formally constituted God's chosen people, remained forever in the
Israelite memory as the outstanding proof and expression
of God's concern, love and almighty power. Here he showed
himself in the clearest possible way to be a living, acting
God, the saviour of his people. Already in the preparation
for this great event he reveals himself to Moses as the God
of Abraham, the God of Isaac and the God of Jacob[6] – here
was no abstract definition or teaching about his nature, but
an evocation of his dealings in the past with the founders of
the race. This is followed by a statement of his interest in
the present sufferings of Israel and a promise of help. As he
had shown himself in the past, so he will show himself in
the future: in his mighty deeds Israel will experience and
come to know him:

> I have seen the affliction of my people who are in Egypt
> and have heard their cry because of their task masters;
> I know their sufferings and I have come down to deliver
> them out of the hands of the Egyptians and to bring them
> up out of that land to a good and broad land, a land
> flowing with milk and honey, the place of the Canaanites,
> the Hittites, the Amorites, the Perizzites, the Hivites and
> the Jebusites. And now, behold, the cry of the people of
> Israel has come to me and I have seen the oppression

---

[5] *Dei Verbum*, art. 2.
[6] *Exod.* 3:6.

with which the Egyptians oppress them. Come, I will send you to Pharaoh that you may bring forth my people, the sons of Israel, out of Egypt.[7]

A little later we read:

I have heard the groaning of the people of Israel whom the Egyptians hold in bondage and I have remembered my covenant. Say, therefore, to the people of Israel, 'I am the Lord and I will bring you out from under the burdens of the Egyptians and I will deliver you from their bondage, and I will redeem you with an outstretched arm and with great acts of judgement, and I will take you for my people, and I will be your God; and you shall know that I am the Lord your God, who has brought you out from under the burdens of the Egyptians.'[8]

When the promised liberation has taken place and Israel has seen the wonderful deeds of God, its thanksgiving and admiration find eloquent expression in the Canticle of Moses. The prophetic understanding of the author explains to the people the significance of what has happened. It is not due to any accident, a mere stroke of fortune, that Israel has been rescued, but to the mighty act of its God. Things might have turned out otherwise, but Yahweh intervened and all obstacles crumbled before his will:

I will sing to the Lord, for he has triumphed gloriously;
the horse and his rider he has thrown into the sea.
The Lord is my strength and my song,
and he has become my salvation;
This is my God and I will praise him,
my father's God and I will exalt him.
The Lord is a man of war;
the Lord is his name.

---

[7]*Exod.* 3:7-10.
[8]*Exod.* 6:5-7.

Pharaoh's chariots and his host he cast into the sea;
and his picked officers are sunk in the Red Sea.
The floods cover them;
and they went down into the depths like a stone.
Thy right hand, oh Lord, shatters the enemy.[9]

The image of God portrayed in these verses remained
indelibly imprinted on the Hebrew consciousness. He was
their Lord, king, protector, faithful ally, mighty champion.
Later they were to learn more about him: through the
Covenant, which revealed him as not only faithful and
merciful, but as holy and demanding holiness and fidelity
in his people; through the prophets, who testified to his
demand for sincere worship and just conduct; through their
own experience as a people, with its alternating triumphs
and disasters, depending on their fidelity or infidelity to him
who was the Lord of history. Again and again the law of
God's self-disclosure manifested in the Exodus was repeated:
God acts, and in his acts he becomes known. According to
many modern scholars, this idea is conveyed in the very name
which God revealed to Moses when Moses asked who he
would tell the Israelites had sent him. This name, Yahweh,
which has traditionally been rendered, 'I am who am', and
taken simply as an affirmation of God's self-existence, is,
according to these scholars, better rendered, 'I shall be
what I shall be', or 'I am becoming what I am becoming',
or, perhaps, 'I shall become with you'. It is not necessary to
exclude from this statement all reference to God's sovereign,
absolutely independent existence; but the primary idea
seems to be that only through the actions which he is about
to do will his name, that is, in Hebrew idiom, his true
nature, be made known. It is his will that Israel should
invoke him by those attributes which are to be manifested
in his dealings with them. Thus invoked, he will answer, and
it is in this sense that he allows them to call him Yahweh.
There is here, according to the mentality of the time, for

---

[9]*Exod.* 15:1-6.

which knowledge of a person's name implied an understanding of his personality, and therefore a certain power
over him, an implicit promise that if they will attend to his
character as he makes himself known in his dealings with
them, and behave towards him appropriately, he will be
at their disposal when they call on him.[10]

In addition to the acts of God there are also his words – or,
rather, there are the human words in which his word finds
expression. This happens through the prophets, God's chosen
spokesmen, who, having been granted a special insight into
God's plan, or even, perhaps, having themselves heard God
speak to them in human words, as Moses did on Mount
Horeb, announce to the people what they have come to
know. As the passage quoted above from the Constitution
on Divine Revelation explains, their words complement
God's acts in history. Impressive and eloquent as the latter
are, they need words to explain them fully – just as, on a
smaller, merely human scale, a gesture of greeting like a
hand-shake is made more meaningful by the words that
accompany it. Only in the combination of act and word is
God's plan truly made manifest, the word excelling in
intelligibility, the act in impact and splendour. In this way
act and word are always linked in the process of revelation.
Neither is to be seen in isolation: otherwise the word
becomes detached from God, whose own eternal word it
expresses, and is seen simply as the vehicle of a doctrine,
while the act loses its meaning and is reduced to the level
of mere magic.

Revelation as Call of God

Up to this point we have been engaged in a rather general
survey of the manner of God's self-disclosure to man. This
has already taught us something about God's purpose in
revealing himself and about the relationship thereby

---

[10]Cf. G. A. F. Knight, *A Christian Theology of the Old Testament*, London
1964, 42.

established between him and man. A closer look at that relationship is now called for. We must ask what it means for man to be addressed by God. The answer to this question will take us to the heart of what revelation means, and give us fresh cause for wonder that so central a reality should have had to wait so long in the ante-rooms of theological discussion.

The first point to be noted is that in revelation God is addressing man. God's word is a call, demanding our response. The beginnings of a dialogue have been established by God's initiative, and it is for man to accept the advances made to him. To God's offer of love man must reply by faith, obedience and a return of love. From now on he can never be the same again. For he cannot ignore the inter-personal relationship which God has created. He cannot pretend that he has not heard; if he tries to do so he is thereby rejecting God's offer of friendship. Whatever course man now takes, a drama of tremendous significance, involving his definitive personal destiny, is due to unfold.[11]

This is something that the celebrated German Protestant theologian, Rudolf Bultmann, has clearly grasped. No one has expressed so powerfully what may be called the existential character of God's meeting with man. This meeting, Bultmann insists, brooks no evasion or delay: a question has been put to man which calls for an answer here and now, an immediate decision, and on this decision hangs the issue of happiness or damnation, fulfilment or frustration, life or death. If man responds in faith, he is freed for authentic personal existence; if he refuses this response, he shuts himself up in his own selfishness and condemns himself to isolation, loneliness and self-destruction.

Clearly, in the face of divine revelation, there is no room for the attitude of the detached observer. Reason certainly demands that the act of faith be preceded by a prudent judgement that God has indeed spoken. But there is no

---

[11] Cf. R. Latourelle, *The Theology of Revelation* (E. tr. New York 1966), 315-20.

escaping a decision about faith, that is, about an absolute
personal commitment to divine love. 'The obedience of faith
(*Rom.* 16:26; cf. 1:5; 2 *Cor.* 10:5-6)', says the Constitution on
Divine Revelation, 'must be given to God who reveals, an
obedience by which a man entrusts his whole self freely to
God.'[12]

The Communication of a Message

There is another aspect of divine revelation, however, one
to which Bultmann, unfortunately, is far from doing justice.
Revelation is not *only* a call to self-commitment; it is *also*
the communication of a message. It imparts objective truth,
what in fact is rightly called doctrine. Because this element
of revelation has tended to receive exclusive emphasis in the
past, it does not follow that it may now be called in question
or neglected. It must indeed be obvious that, by the very
fact of speaking to man and making him an offer of friendship, God is telling man something about himself. The offer of
personal communion is itself an implicit statement that God
is a loving God. In fact it is precisely in God's concern for
man and his plan to save him that the revealed message
essentially consists. Explicit teaching about this plan is
certainly given, but not as something to be considered in
isolation from God's actual calling and saving. As already
explained, words and acts form a unity. Hence, there can
be no question of reducing the Christian message to a mere
set of propositions, of abstract statements about God. But
neither can the intellectual content of revelation be allowed
to evaporate into 'pure existential encounter'. This would
be to neglect both the objective meaning of God's word and
the aspirations of man's intellectual nature.

If one wished to sum up the message imparted by God in
revelation, one could scarcely find a better idea than that
of the 'mystery', proclaimed by St Paul in the epistle to the
Ephesians.[13] The 'mystery', in the special sense in which

---

[12]*Dei Verbum*, art 5.
[13]*Eph.* 1:9-10.

Paul uses it, is nothing other than God's plan of salvation, kept secret from the beginning but now revealed by and in Christ. From all eternity it has been God's purpose to unite all men to himself through the merits and after the pattern of Christ, his Son. Here, the entire system of salvation and its significance are concisely stated. Around this central affirmation all the great truths of revelation, the mysteries of Christianity in the more usual sense of that phrase, are clustered; indeed, they are already implied in it. The doctrines of the blessed Trinity, incarnation, and redemption, for example, are presupposed in God's decree raising up sinful man, through the power of the holy Spirit, to be conformable to the image of his only-begotten Son. Similarly, the doctrine of the Church is a statement of God's plan to gather all men into one great society of the saved, of which the visible Church on earth is the expression and preparation. The doctrine of the Last Things is also implied in the same central affirmation: God's plan reaches its final fulfilment in the possession of eternal glory by those who have been found worthy, and this, of course, inevitably means the definitive exclusion from the kingdom of all others. In fact, there is no part of Christian doctrine which is not firmly grounded in the unique 'mystery' of salvation. In revealing himself as the God of love, as the saving God who, in Christ, comes with an offer of fellowship to man held captive by sin, God has already said in embryo all that the Church and her theology will later spell out in particular and detailed teachings.

The Self-Disclosure of God

Revelation, then, is both a call to man and a teaching about God. It is also a self-disclosure of God. This aspect has already emerged to some extent, but a few further remarks on it are called for. The very fact that God speaks to man inevitably involves some revelation of himself. All speech is revealing of the speaker, even if it reveals no more than the desire to enter into communication. As a rule

speech reveals more than this: it expresses a desire of the
speaker, his will that something be done, his belief that
something is true, etc. At its highest, however, speech is the
expression of love. It unveils to another, as only speech can,
a person's inner thoughts and dispositions, with a view to
sharing them. It offers a gift of all that is most inward and
personal in the life of the speaker, and invites a similar gift
in return. It expresses, in short, a genuine gift of self, which,
if accepted, leads to a communion in love, a real sharing of
life.[14] We see this very clearly in marriage. The union of
two people in married love presupposes and fosters a community of mind and heart in which each discloses his inner
spiritual world to the other. The physical union is secondary
to this, though it is a powerful expression of it and means
of promoting it. The result of this profound sharing by the
partners is a certain fusion or intermingling, limited but
real, of the two personalities. And the more communication
there is in marriage, through conversation and otherwise,
the more love will grow. On the other hand, when communication ceases, when the parties have nothing to say to
each other, or at any rate no longer have any meaning for
each other, their union has lost its value and its true cohesive
force.

Making all the necessary qualifications and observing all
due proportions, a similar relationship arises when God
speaks his word to man. God makes known to man his inner
life; he discloses to him the secrets of his being. It thereby
becomes possible for man to share God's inmost being,
though, if he is to do so in fact, he will have to accept the
gift that is offered, yield himself to the attraction which the
gift exercises upon him from the first moment that it is
offered. Granted this initial response from man – in itself
evidently a gift or grace from God – God's loving action
will invade his whole personality and take him into fellowship of life, thereby raising him to a new, unheard-of plane

---

[14]Cf. Latourelle, *op. cit.*, 319.

of existence. This is what theology means when it speaks of
the sanctifying grace which comes into the soul through
justifying faith, or of the supernatural life to which man is
raised up by Christ. This is what St John is referring to,
when he says that eternal life consists in the knowledge of
God and Jesus Christ.[15] Eternal life is precisely such knowledge, but, as will be evident from what has been said, the
knowledge in question is not a purely intellectual matter.
It involves also a moral attitude, a willingness to accept
fellowship with God. It includes a basic option for the truth
which God has revealed and which he is.

The delicate personal relationship here involved and the
need for a fitting attitude on man's part in the face of God's
approach to him are seen more clearly when we recall that
God's revealing word has the character of testimony. God,
that is to say, asks man to accept a revelation on his personal
authority. Man has no other evidence for it; he can know it
only by accepting God's word. Obviously God is here
showing confidence in man – otherwise he would not think
of revealing himself to him – and is inviting confidence in
return, confidence in God's truthfulness and loving designs
towards man. If man shows this confidence, he is giving
honour to God, acknowledging him as the God of truth and
love.[16] Man's fundamental moral attitudes are evidently
deeply involved here. All depends on whether he is willing
to accept God as the focus and centre of his life. Unless
man, in other words, has at least some beginning of love of
God in his heart, he will not accept the offer of friendship
God makes to him in revelation.

Interpersonal Communion Effectively Realized
From the above analysis of revelation it will be clear that
it is quite a complex reality. While our initial definition of
revelation as God making himself known to man, still
stands, it evidently implies much more than first impressions

[15] *John* 17:3.
[16] Cf. Latourelle, *op. cit.*, 320-4.

might lead one to suppose. In particular, it involves a radical transformation of man, provided he accepts it, and in any case it affects him profoundly. Since, strictly speaking, revelation occurs only when man accepts it, it is more adequately defined in terms of an interpersonal exchange. Revelation is God entering into communion of love and knowledge with man and thereby raising man to the level of his own inner life. 'Through this revelation, therefore', states the Constitution on Divine Revelation, 'the invisible God (cf. *Col.* 1:15; 1 *Tim.* 1:17) out of the abundance of his love speaks to men as friends (cf. *Ex.* 33:11; *Gen.* 15:14-15) and lives among them (cf. *Bar.* 3:38), so that he may invite and take them into fellowship with himself.'[17]

Another point, also implicit in what has been said, deserves to be highlighted. When God speaks, his word, as Scripture says, does not return to him unfulfilled. Even a human word can be an instrument carrying out the will of the speaker, in a command, for example, or request. Whereas a human word, however, may fail in its purpose, God's word, though it does not do violence to the human will and often meets with opposition and may seem frustrated, cannot ultimately be defeated in its purpose. This follows from the fact that God's word is the expression of his will, and while this will, as addressed to each individual person, is conditional on a free response, God remains the master of events and gradually brings to completion his grand design. The power inherent in God's word is shown, on the one hand, in the mighty acts which attend the proclamation of his will and bring his will to pass; on the other hand, in the interior attraction which God exercises on the human heart. Through this twofold efficacy the word of God, sooner or later, achieves its goal: salvation occurs, the elect are gathered in, the kingdom of heaven reaches its full perfection, the revelation which began with Abraham blossoms into that perfect fellowship in which the whole

---

[17]*Dei Verbum*, art 2.

Christ, head and members, is united to the Father in a
blessed eternity of knowledge and love.

Revelation as Historical

A further aspect of revelation as outlined above, one that
receives much attention nowadays, is its historical character.
We have already seen that revelation takes place through a
series of actions and words, but the significance of this has
not been fully brought out. The following points are worth
noting.[18]

First, it is revelation that has endowed history with movement, growth and direction. By pointing to a future time of
fulfilment, first to the coming of the Messiah, and then to
his return in glory at the consummation of all things, it has
rescued man from the meaninglessness of a cyclic view of
time in which the same pattern of events is endlessly repeated.
Here lie the origins of the notion of progress which man,
particularly in our time, finds so dynamic and alluring. The
reason for this fascination is obvious: progress gives meaning
to human history and the events that make it up, and holds
forth the prospect of final success. This is in no small measure
the explanation of the attraction of Marxism for many of our
contemporaries: by holding forth the prospect of the
millennium, of a paradise on earth to which the human
race is moving forward, it meets the human craving for
meaning and direction in life. But it is Christianity that
brought the idea of progress into the world, and Christianity
cannot agree to its being appropriated by others. A better
understanding of revelation can help us to renew our appreciation of its Christian origins, and can instil in us a lively
sense of the movement of history towards the only goal which
God has appointed for it, the return of Christ in glory to
establish his eternal kingdom.

That revelation is historical means yet something more.

---

[18]Cf. Latourelle, *op. cit.*, 343-58.

Revelation is itself a sacred history, a series of events linked together in a unified development in which each plays its part in achieving God's saving plan. It is for this reason that the Exodus, the Covenant and other events of Old Testament history are still significant for us today. They have had a part in shaping us and we cannot fully understand what we are, what God has done and is doing for us in the Church, unless we have some idea of their meaning. The sacrament of baptism, for example, is greatly impoverished if we see it in isolation from the long series of antecedent events, beginning with the Exodus, by which God was effecting the salvation of his people. These events were recapitulated and brought to perfection in the life, death and glorification of Jesus, and now come to fruition for the individual in the regenerating waters of baptism.

There is yet a third sense in which revelation may be said to be historical. It is that revelation takes place *in* and *through* human history. In the very facts and events that make up human life God is revealing himself. In the lives and deaths of men, in their triumphs and defeats, their loves and hates, their vices and virtues, their good and evil deeds, God is speaking, acting, showing himself to man, carrying out his plan, promoting his grand design of forming a people to enter into eternal fellowship with him. This means that temporal events count, that what we do at every moment has profound and eternal consequences, that all that happens on this earth is in some sense permanent. For many of our contemporaries the happenings of human life lack ultimate seriousness: they pass, and cease to be, and sooner or later are forgotten. In Buddhism, one of the great religions of the world, even though man's future destiny is linked to good actions, all life on earth is held to be a mere shadow of reality and the virtuous life consists in realizing and coming to terms with this fact. But Judaism and Christianity are emphatic on the unseen depths of the events of human history and their eternal consequences, and they owe this emphasis to God's self-disclosure in and through the history of the Israel-

ites.[19] The well-known Christian teaching on 'the sacrament
of the present moment', with its stress on the irreplaceable
significance of even the smallest occasion in human life, is
a striking illustration of the great practical significance of
the fact that God has given himself to man in a historical
revelation.

The Fullness of Revelation

Revelation, we have seen, is a continuing process. At a
certain point, however, the process reaches fulfilment. There
comes a moment in history when God has fully revealed and
given himself to man. This moment is ushered in by the
incarnation, by the appearance on earth in human form
of God's eternal, substantial Word. In Jesus Christ the perfect
exchange between God and man is established, and from
him this fellowship spreads out to embrace the entire world.

God's word, let us recall, is the expression of God himself. As such it has only one perfect and archetypal realisa-
tion, namely the Word who has proceeded from the Father
from eternity and, in common with the Father, possesses
the fullness and perfection of the Godhead. All other
utterances of God, in whatever form – creative acts, historical
deeds and events, human words – are instruments and
reflections of this one, substantial Word. In Jesus Christ
the one Word of the Father becomes present and visible in
our world. In him therefore the entire being of the Father is
expressed and revealed. In him all that has been said above
about revelation is fully and uniquely verified: about revelation as the voice of the one true God, the living God,
sounding in man's ears; about the expression of revelation
in human words and mighty deeds of salvation; about the
call thereby addressed to man and the response that is
required of him; about the 'mystery' or hidden plan of God
which revelation makes public; about the self-disclosure of
God in a loving, confiding, trusting gesture aimed at setting

----

[19]Cf. Moran, *op. cit.*, 42-3.

up an intimate fellowship with man; about revelation as
historical, as something that gives meaning and direction
to human life, that unfolds in a unified series of events, and
is incarnate in the conditions of man's existence. In the
person, life, death and glorification of Jesus all this is
manifestly and supremely present. In his words, his preaching, his calling and training of his disciples, his life of prayer
and penance, his miracles, his conflicts with the Jewish
leaders, his relations with his family and friends, above all
in the great act of redeeming love which ended and crowned
his earthly life – in a word, in everything he did and all he
was – Christ made known the Father and brought to fulfilment the Father's plan to unite mankind in a communion
of love and knowledge with himself. 'He who sees me sees
the Father' (*John* 14:9): in these words of Jesus to Philip
summed up the absolutely supreme and central role Christ
plays in the history of revelation.[20]

It is plain that this role of Christ has depths which it is
impossible to sound. Perhaps the best summary of what is
implied is to be found in another celebrated statement of
Christ, also reported by St John: 'I am the way, and the
truth, and the life' (*John* 14:6). In these simple words we
are taught not only the true significance of revelation – it
is not merely truth but life as well – and the exclusive role
of Christ in bringing it to us, but also the necessity of personal
union with Christ in order to share in it. To appreciate the
full significance of this, we must observe that it is in the
person of Christ that revelation in its fullness has occurred.
It is not just that the Son of God appeared on earth and
announced God's word to the human race. What has
happened rather is that the Son of God has become incarnate in an individual man and that revelation, therefore, has
occurred first of all in this man's human consciousness. The
man Christ, whose integral manhood implies genuine human
knowledge, is the first recipient of God's full self-disclosure

---

[20]Cf. *Dei Verbum*, art 4.

C

in the word that has become incarnate in him. The perfect
fellowship with the human race that God has willed to
establish has now become a reality. In Christ God discloses
and gives himself fully to a member of our race and meets
with a total response, of which the supreme act of loving
obedience on the cross is the perfect expression. In that act
the union of love between God and the human race in which
revelation is accomplished is established definitively and in
its fullness. In and through his gesture of complete self-
surrender to the Father, Jesus gives the final expression and
proof of his filial love, thereby attaining, in his human
consciousness, to that complete and untrammelled union
with the Father which belongs to him as the eternal Son.
Now is fulfilled the prayer he uttered to the Father shortly
before he died: 'Now, Father, glorify thou me in thy own
presence with the glory which I had with thee before the
world was made' (*John* 17:5). It is nothing else than the
fullness of revelation that Jesus prays for here: the 'glory'
he asks to receive is the bliss of intimate fellowship with the
Father through knowledge and love, without the limitations
which the conditions of this worldly existence had hitherto
imposed.[21]

On the cross this ultimate break-through, this consummation, was accomplished. But for the moment its true character
remained hidden, its glorious effects unrealized. Only with
the resurrection does Christ arrive at the summit of his way,
receiving in body and soul the full effects of perfect fellowship with the Father. It is at this moment that revelation
is perfectly accomplished: in this mighty deed, the supreme
act of God's saving love for his people, and in the light with
which it floods the human soul of Christ, the long course of
God's revelatory activity reaches its culmination.[22]

In the risen Christ revelation is present in its fullness. The
whole subsequent course of God's saving plan is determined

[21]See the excellent chapter on Christ as Revelatory Communion in Moran,
op. cit., 57-76.
    [22]*Ibid.*, 71-4

by this fact. Henceforward, all that remains is that, by faith and the sacraments, men should share in the knowledge and love of Christ. It is in and through the risen Christ, and only in this way, that they can respond to the advances of God. It is for this purpose that Christ has instituted the Church, committing to it his word and his sacraments, the means by which his Spirit comes to dwell in men's hearts. Through the Spirit the revelation which was begun in Old Testament times and reached its fullness in the risen Christ becomes a living reality in the community of the Church, God's people. Living the life of the Spirit, the life of the new, Christian man, the believer makes his way to the final consummation, to the full and definitive sharing in the life of the risen Christ.

Morality:
Man's response to God

Enda McDonagh

God's self-communication to men, which is called divine revelation, was not simply to give man information about God. In communicating himself in this way God sought a relationship with man. He offered himself to man out of love, asking for man's loving response. This loving response is the supreme task of man's life. So human living and behaviour or morality must be described in the light of divine revelation as the living out of this relationship, as man's response to the divine invitation.

The invitation-response structure of revelation itself is very evident in the standard account of it given in the Bible. By entering human history and speaking to man God created this situation of relationship. He invited man from the very beginning, as the book of Genesis records, to a life of intimacy with himself. And despite man's initial failure to respond, God persisted in pursuing the relationship through the history of Israel to the sending of his own son. The successive interventions of God in human history are directed towards establishing a loving union between God and his people, whereby he would be their God and they would be and live as his people. The agreements or covenants, to use the technical term, which God makes with his people through Noah, Abraham and, above all, Moses, are further stages in this relationship. They involve God's self-giving to man out of love and ask for man's loving response in the gift of himself and his life.

They have an invitation-response structure. Revelation as God's self-gift or *donum* expresses an invitation, demands a response. It is also a *mandatum*. The terms of the invitation are spelled out most explicitly in the Mosaic Covenant which forms the centre of and gives its name to the whole preparatory stage of God's self-communication to man. The Mosaic Law, and especially the Ten Commandments, forms the written concrete expression of the response demanded of God's people in consequence of God's giving of himself to them. The Commandments are not to be seen then as imposed separately, but as arising from the self-gift of God which transforms this people into his people who must now live as his people.

This was however a preparatory stage. A new covenant was promised through the prophets Jeremiah and Ezechiel which would be the full and proper expression of God's relationship with his people. It would also involve, of course, a covenant morality or law, a fuller and deeper response appropriate to the fuller and deeper self-giving of God. It would be a covenant written primarily not on tablets of stone but on men's hearts.

The concrete expression of the New Covenant was a person, the God-man Jesus Christ in his life, death and resurrection. God's self-giving to man reached its climax in his becoming man. By entering the human condition, sharing human nature, becoming life to men in all things except sin, God communicated himself fully to man. No fuller communication is possible in our earthly state, no fuller revelation.

The final stage of the historical revelation was a completion, a fulfilment, not a destruction. It had the same covenant invitation-response structure. God gave himself to man that man might give himself to God. The self-giving of God was at the same time a call to man to respond. A new and definite stage in the God-man relationship was reached. And all this was realized in Jesus Christ.

In shaping man's moral response to the divine invitation Jesus Christ forms the key-figure, the centre about which all the rest turns. Through his divine-human reality he is at once the fullness of the divine invitation and of the human response. God's fullness of communication to man in becoming man is complemented in Jesus by man's fullness of response to God. The incarnation, God entering the human condition, committing himself in his sheer divinity to man, is complemented by the human life of Christ which was obedient to the Father to the point of death. The Word who was God and who was made flesh, who was the Father's only-begotten Son in whom he was well pleased, who reflects the glory of God and bears the very stamp of his nature, to whom all power in heaven and earth was given, became for all men the way, the truth and the life, through whom alone men might come to God, in whom alone they could bear fruit, have life, be called and be sons of the Father.

The incarnation of the Son of God completed in the glorification of the man Jesus Christ when the human was fully penetrated by the divine, established Christ as the head of the human race, the new Adam. In him all men share in principle in the divine sonship. To this they are called. As sons they must behave. The way of behaviour or the morality enshrined in Christ as invitation and response, as the Covenant or New Law, is a morality of sonship. Whatever expresses this sonship in Christ is morally good, whatever frustrates or is opposed to it is morally bad.

This sonship is not to be understood as something external to men, something attributed to them by a kind of legal fiction as if God had decided to call men his sons without that affecting them in any radical way. The incarnation indicates the radical character of his sonship. Man has become a sharer in the divine nature through God sharing in the human nature. And man's entry into the divine nature has been achieved at the level of the Son. It is as sons of the Father that they are 'divinized', sharers in the sonship of the second person of the Trinity. And they receive this through the gift of the Spirit, who is the mutual love of Father and Son. The role of the Spirit in the divine plan of salvation and in the individual Christian life tends to be obscured, at least partly, because he has not a personal image in the sense of the Father and the Son and so is not so easily pictured in his personal activity. Yet in the New Testament his activity emerges at key-points. By his power the Virgin Mary was over-shadowed at the incarnation. At the opening of his public mission of preaching the kingdom, Jesus was led by the Spirit into the desert and the Spirit descended upon him in the form of a dove at his baptism by John. His imminent death he explained to his disciples as necessary that he might send the Spirit. And the sending of the Spirit at Pentecost transformed a haphazard collection of disciples into the dynamic community of the Church through whom all men would come to Christ. By the power of the Spirit given at baptism the individual is incorporated into Christ, given a share of his sonship, and enabled to understand and respond to the Father's call. In his life as a whole, in each moral area of that life and in each individual situation, the Christian is led by the Spirit to understand and respond to the Father's call, to do what is demanded of him as a sharer in the divine sonship of Christ.

The fullness of God's self-communication to man revealed him as tripersonal. When the personal relationship which God initiated with man developed into its new stage at the incarnation the personal reality of God emerged as that of three persons in one God. The three persons have their distinctive role in the development of this relationship with mankind as a whole, in salvation history. It is the Father, the source or principle within the Godhead, who is the initiator of the plan. From the Old Testament, preparatory stage when God is evident and active as a personal reality, but not yet as a tripersonal reality, the transition to the New is made most easily by defining this personal author of salvation as God the Father. The God (*ho Theos*) of the New Testament is above all the Father and in this role in continuity with Yahweh of the people of Israel. But he can only appear as God the Father in conjunction with the appearance of God the Son. It is only as the divine sonship of Jesus Christ emerges, that strictly speaking the divine fatherhood can emerge.

It is however the Father of our Lord Jesus Christ, in the strictest and divine sense, who implements the plan of salvation outlined in the Old Testament, by sending his only-begotten Son. And the plan is completed by the return of the Son made man to his Father, expressed in the glorification of the Son in his human nature, the full penetration of the human by the divine which enables the Son also in his human condition to be, with the Father, the source of the gift of the Spirit to mankind. By this gift all men share in the divine sonship, and while remaining truly human as Jesus was, become 'divinized', sharers in the divine nature in a real sense.

Revelation, salvation history, whatever one calls it, is the extension and actualization of the inner trinitarian divine life in creation, in humanity. The indwelling of the Trinity, the union with the tripersonal God, constitutes the basis of all human living and behaviour. Christian morality then as the human response to this divine gift has an inbuilt trinitarian structure which arises from the personal relationship which each man enjoys with the three divine persons. It is not strictly correct in this context to speak of relationship to the three persons by appropriation, the technical term whereby a particular created reality, properly speaking the result of a common divine activity, is ascribed through some external property to one or other person. The divine indwelling or the correlative expression of the same reality, the admission of man to the divine life as a son of the Father, means that man is no longer simply a created reality, no longer a work external to the divinity in that sense, an *opus ad extra.* In a very real sense he is *ad intra,* enjoying a real share in the divine life and so in the divine relationships.

The trinitarian character of Christian living makes clear the basic unity between liturgy and life, prayer and work, religious and profane activity. Liturgical prayer is directed to the Father. It can only however be prayer to the Father by union with the only-begotten Son. Through his humanity all men are empowered to address his Father as their Father. Through the sacramental realization of his giving himself totally to the Father in his life, death and resurrection, men are brought into perceptible human contact with the exercise of divine sonship in human form. Their sonship is of value only as a share in Christian sonship. Their acknowledgement of the Father is of value only as a share in his. Their prayer must be his prayer.

So the Church prays to the Father through Christ his Son and this is made possible by the Spirit of sonship who is poured forth into men's hearts and by whom they cry 'Abba, Father!' Prayer forms a particular and explicit realization of their living relationship with the personal God. The relationship itself, like the husband and wife or parent-child relationship, is a permanent reality which underlies and structures all human living. So what man does explicitly at prayer, responding to the Father through the Son by the power of the holy Spirit, he does implicitly in his other human activity. Each situation involving a moral decision incorporates a call from the Father. The response of the Christian should be that of a son, modelled on the filial response of the only-begotten Son and grounded in it. To understand the call and be capable of the response he needs the light and strength of the Spirit. In life as in liturgy human activity should recognize and realize this trinitarian structure. It is the failure to behave as a son with consequent disruption of the true relations to the three persons that constitutes sin.

Jesus Christ in his humanity and divinity provides the concrete example as well as the living source of every man's relations with God. One is a Christian at all by acceptance

of his central role. Faithful to the New Testament account
of how he acquired his first disciples, a Christian in the
current usage of the term means a follower of Christ. This
following began as a simple response to his summons to the
disciples on the shore of the Sea of Galilee and developed
through a literal, physical following of him to the complete
acceptance of his claims and his teaching. It meant too a
shaping of his destiny and of the self-giving to the Father
which that involved by taking up the cross and becoming
obedient even unto death. The following and imitation of
himself which Christ demands in the New Testament should
permeate one's whole life to the very surrender of that life.
To be a follower of Christ then demands a Christlike response
to a given situation. This is the test of morality for Christians,
to behave as Christ would. To do this one must understand
or put on the mind of Christ, St Paul reminds his readers.

The test itself may seem somewhat impractical to many,
and indeed its content has to be filled out in a way that will
be pointed out later. But given some basic Christian education the application of this test in a particular situation
could yield some very concrete, if occasionally disturbing
conclusions. It may be unconscious fear of being disturbed
that has led many people to make a sharp distinction between
ordinary morality and the call to Christian perfection,
leading to what is sometimes called a two-storey morality,
which is in no way based on the New Testament. There is
only one call, to follow Christ, and it is a call to perfection,
a goal to be aimed at rather than achieved, as will appear,
but one to be aimed at by all and in each concrete situation.

For the Christian the standard or norm of morality is the
person Jesus Christ. In passing it might be remarked that
there are no greater difficulties about accepting a person as
norm than about accepting an abstraction like human nature
or an indefinable like the divine will or the greatest happiness
of the greatest number. When that person is the son of God
made man, accessible to all men in his divine-human
reality, the difficulty may be less.

The pattern of Christ's personal response to the Father recorded for us in the New Testament together with his explicit moral directives interpreting this response, fill out in a rich way the content of the following of Christ for man. However, it is necessary to take the argument a stage further to see how Christ's person and teaching combine more deeply as man's norm.

The invitation expressed in and by Christ was not simply to follow him, to share his ideals, even his destiny, but to share his very being, as the man who was the Son of God. It is to be sons of the Father as he was that men are summoned. Their full being involves a human nature, but also a participation in the divine being. By this participation they become sons because it is a participation in Christ, in the Son. They must be branches of the vine which is Christ, members of the body which is Christ. They must live 'in Christ', a phrase that is almost an obsession with St Paul. As life issues in activity so the life of Christ that is in them, the life of the Son of God made man must issue in their activity. Whatever activity then expresses this life is good and Christian activity, the activity proper to a follower of Christ. Whatever activity frustrates or destroys this life is bad, unchristian activity.

If the venerable moral axiom, *actio sequitur esse* (as a being is, so should it act), is to be invoked, it must be applied to the being that is there, the full being of the Christian, of man called to share in Christ's being and be a son of the Father. The being then is both divine and human. It is ultimately the being of the Son of God made man, because even in his human nature he is the head and standard of the race, indeed the foundation of our very humanity. So in his divinity and humanity he possesses the being in which all men participate and which in this metaphyisical union proves the determinant of their behaviour. *Actio sequitur esse* should be properly understood. For man called in Christ to be a son of the Father it reads *actio sequitur esse Christianum* or *esse Christi* or *esse filii incarnati*. It is the full Christian being

of each man derived from Christ or the Son incarnate which
is in question.

Recognizing Christ as he is, man must follow him in
everything he does, even to death, seeing that all human
activity must express the Christ-life in each man and that
man's true being is human and called to share in the divine
sonship. With man's being so founded in Christ it becomes
intelligible to say that Christ is the norm or standard of
morality. However, to clarify this further some characteristics of this norm or standard call for discussion.

The norm of Christian behaviour is primarily something
internal to man, affecting him from within. In this it con-
trasts with any proposed or imposed set of rules to which a
man should conform. Christian morality consists primarily
not in such a set of rules, but in man's share in the call and
reality of Christ as Son of the Father become man. The call
and reality form the covenant which Jeremiah said should
be written not in tablets of stone but in the hearts of men.
To speak of a law for Christian behaviour is to use the
word in an analogical sense, a sense proportionate to but
not identical with the sense of the word in civil or canon
law, where it is a precisely formulated rational prescription
imposed on man from the outside by the due authority for
the common welfare. The Christian moral 'law' arises from
within, as the expression of his sonship of the Father in his
human condition.

To be the object of human understanding or discourse
at all, this internal reality must be formulated at least to
the extent of saying that the being of the Son of God made
man is the standard or norm. And the implications of this
require further formulation which has been accomplished
in fair measure by Jesus himself in the Gospels and by his
disciples. The self communication of God to man has
necessarily sought expression in human language and so
has the response from man which that communication
involves. Jesus explained for us the central divine reality
and the terms of human response which he incorporated

in his person, life and death. The New Testament writings
provide a written account of the meaning and chief demands
of Christian living. St Thomas points out, the 'New Law' is
also a 'written law'.

As a written law it is the attempt to express the reality
internal to man, the call to divine sonship in human form,
in some verbal formulas. Such formulas are necessary and
originate with Christ himself and the New Testament. They
are, however, secondary to the internal reality and never in
fact completely express it. They are always approximate and
capable of fuller and better expression. God's self-
communication in Christ can never be exhaustively expressed in human terms. This applies to the doctrinal or
dogmatic formulations of the New Testament and later
Church teaching. Revelation is primarily a living reality, the
Son of God made man, and does not yield to any total verbal
exposition. This does not destroy the value of verbal exposition or make it less necessary. It simply underlines its
limitations. It is true as far as it goes but it is not the primary
reality and can never replace it or describe it fully.

The doctrinal or dogmatic expression of revelation as
God's self-giving to man in Christ is only complete when
that revelation is understood as an invitation to man.
Revelation as an invitation or a way of life for man is
expressed in formulas with only the same limited validity.
There can be no question then of a precise Christian or
divine code of law which embraces all the situations in a
man's life and which he only has to obey. Definite formulations have been given. They are clear if not always precise.
The most famous and basic of these is Christ's own summary
of morality as 'Thou shalt love God and thou shalt love thy
neighbour'. Further formulation of the way of life in Christ
may be found in the New Testament and in the Old as
related to the New. The Church in its mission of preaching
Christ expounds this way of life authoritatively and in
greater detail as it applies to general or more particular
situations. And all these formulations are true and helpful,

but they are not the primary reality or its total content.
Christian morality is not primarily a code of law, but a
person, Jesus Christ, whose human and divine being man
shares and should develop. This sharing is internal to man,
but does however require some external formulation.

As a second characteristic of Christian morality, it is
worth considering its relational character. It is a morality
of relationships, that is to say, it is founded on certain
relationships and is a call to develop them.

Revelation itself is God's invitation to man to enter into
a relationship with him. God gives himself to man that man
may give himself to God. The development of this God-
man relationship, which issued in the incarnation, specified
man's relation to God more exactly by relating him to God
as trinitarian. So man became a son of the Father in Christ
by the gift of the Spirit. And Christian morality is living
out the relationships with the three Divine Persons.

However, the self-communication of God was not to man
as an isolated individual, but to man as the community or
relational reality that he is at the human level. It was to a
people that God communicated himself, and it is in a people,
God's people, that the individual must respond. This is God
respecting man's community dimension. It is through a
community of at least two people, and as a result of their
relationship, that a man comes into the world. It is through
his relations with these two people and the wider community
to which they belong, that he develops as a human being.
Physically, emotionally, intellectually, religiously, his personal maturity may be assessed through his capacity for and
realization of relationships with other people. In relationships he actualizes his highest personal capacity, his capacity
to love.

The incarnation and redemption manifest and make
possible human relationships in all their grandeur. It is as
sons of the Father that the community bond between men
as brothers is properly understood and finally possible.
Salvation-history or the redemptive work of the Trinity is

directed to communion of all men in sonship of the Father
and brotherhood between one another. The task imposed
and the response demanded by revelation is the building of
this community, the development of these filial and fraternal
relationships.

In the light of this internal reality of man's single relationship to God and his fellowman, Christ could formulate the
essence of Christian morality in the command to love God
and to love our neighbour. St Paul could insist on the
primacy of charity, reducing all the commandments to it.
And St John could proclaim the unified reality which they
express when he denied that any man could love God
without loving his neighbour. And if God in his self-
revelation constitutes man's moral life, then both commands
can be summed up as the New Testament sums them up
in the one word, love.

God then allows man to share and live his own reality, the
trinitarian life, divine love. This pinpoints a third and very
mysterious characteristic of Christian morality, that it is a
divine-human reality. God admits man, as has been pointed
out, to a share in his own divine nature. Yet in all this he
respects man's humanity. In speaking to man, in entering
into a relationship with him, God transforms man, raises
him above the level of creature to draw him into the divine
relationships and the divine life, but he does not absorb
him. To do so would result in pantheism, destroy the
possibility of a genuine God-man relationship and make
nonsense of the incarnation. Man remains fully man in his
relationship with God, even as Christ was fully man. It is
through his human condition and by developing its potenti-
alities that man realizes his sonship of God. The divine
invitation which forms the moral character of a Christian
and which was expressed in the person of Christ consists
precisely in living out the divine sonship in the human
condition. But the human condition is an essential part of
man's character as it was an essential part of Christ. And
man's invitation or task includes the human as the means of

expressing the divine. So the moral values enshrined in humanity or the moral perfections of which the human being is capable constitute an essential and permanent part of morality for the Christian. Isolated and abstracted from the total Christian reality these values or perfections may be described as 'natural' morality or 'natural' moral law where 'natural' is used in the technical sense of belonging to human nature precisely as human and distinct from its divine complement in the incarnation. So the moral values of the 'natural law' (a most misleading if conventional term) retain their validity in the full Christian order, the only existing order.

Christ as divine self-communication and human response incarnates the existing moral order. And he does so for all men of all time. Yet God's relations with mankind have a history. Christ himself appeared on earth relatively late in the history of mankind and so of its relations with God. Today and for what seems likely to be quite a long time to come, a relatively small number of men acknowledge him in any sense. Can one speak then in any meaningful way of Christ as constituting the one moral norm or moral law for all men?

Briefly, yes. But to do so requires a fairly careful theological statement of Christ's central role in creation and redemption from the very beginning, and the progressive manifestation and realization of that role in the history of mankind.

It may now be seen from the New Testament, I think, that Christ, the God-man, is not only the centre and basis of God's revelation or salvation, but also of creation. Man was created in view of Christ. Humanity was realized because of Christ. It is true that the Second Person, as the Word or Logos, the first and full expression of the divine Godhead, is the source of all other expressions, in particular of that expression we call creation, including man. But this role is not assigned simply to the Logos by St Paul, but to the Word made flesh, to Christ. So man and creation as integrated with and leading to man, derived their created reality from the supreme point of creation to which they led, the man who was a divine person. To him they led, from him they took their meaning. In him they were created. Man was possible, says Karl Rahner in that elliptical way of his, because the incarnation was possible. Or man came into being because of the incarnation, because of the God-man.

In his very humanity then man derives from Christ, certainly as the Logos and in my opinion as the Logos made man. Of course man never existed in his humanity alone. From the beginning he was called to a personal relationship with the divine, to a supernatural mode of existence, to a life of grace. The proper shape of this call only emerged in the course of history. It was of course a call to divine worship, as finally manifested in Jesus Christ.

But the call was there, in virtue of Christ, from the very beginning of all men. The capacity to accept it, based on Christ's acceptance, was also available to all men at all times. Yet the way in which that call was recognized and realized has varied considerably through history. Through a special divine initiative the expression of the call, or God's self-communication to man, assumed a peculiar and developing form in the history of God's chosen people, the Israelites. Their response to that call was made concrete above all in the Mosaic Law, the centre of which was the Ten Commandments. But it took other shapes and forms for other people. St Paul categorically stated that all men before Jesus received this call, and could recognize and respond to it, the Jews in the Law, the non-Jews or Gentiles in the testimony of conscience to the law written in their own being. For the Jews before Jerusalem the Mosaic Law was the appropriate historical realization of the moral order finally manifest in Christ. And it derived all its value from him. It was ultimately transparent of him, transcending itself to reach out to him, fulfilling, in St Paul's phrase, the role of teacher or instructor in leading towards him. For the Gentiles the moral values accessible to them in their

D

human living were also derived from Christ, transparent of
him, leading to him. So it is today that people who do not
recognize Christ explicitly, yet encounter him in the moral
values and possibilities of their actual existence, in the
summons to truth and justice and chastity, in the call to
love and serve the neighbour. It is not explicit recognition
of him that ultimately counts according to his own description of the last judgement, but the response to the call of the
needy which is always the call of Christ.

Christian morality is universal and historical in the
precise sense that Christ is universal and historical. He is the
one mediator for all men yet he appeared at a particular
historical moment. The divine invitation expressed in him
and the human response achieved by him are available to
all men at all times, although their shape and content were
only partially and gradually realized for all men before
him and for many after him.

While Christian morality may be expressed in the form
of a law and formulated as a collection of written prescriptions, it is only analogically and inexactly a law in our sense
and only secondarily written. Properly and primarily it is
the divine self-giving calling for a human response which
was manifested in the person of Jesus Christ and takes place
within each man.

Redemption:
God saves the Sinner

DONAL FLANAGAN

It was his Son that God sent, the Scriptures tell us, born of a woman, made like us that we might receive the adoption of sons (cf. *Gal.* 4:4). We are to be conformed to the image of the Son. The divine love of the Father, wishing to extend itself into the world of men, to draw men into the life of God, will achieve its purpose by the extension of divine sonship to us, his creatures. The Father wills to call all men to be his sons in the likeness of his only-begotten Son. And so he sends him to them to share their condition that they in turn may share his. They are to be sons of the Father in the Son. They are to receive from the Father through the Son the trinitarian Spirit who is the Spirit of the Father and the Spirit of the Son.

Christ, the First-Born

Already in the incarnation itself we are shown man's destiny, our destiny. For Christ is intended by God from eternity as the crowning point of the entire creation. We read in the epistle to the Colossians:

He (Christ) is the image of the invisible God, the first-born of all creation, for in him all things were created in heaven and on earth, visible and invisible, whether thrones or principalities or dominions or powers. All things were

39

created through him and for him. He is before all things
and in him all things hold together. (*Col.* 1:15-16.)

Creation reaches its peak in Christ. In him the potenti-
alities of human nature for union with the divine are realized
fully. In his incarnation God takes hold of man and binds
him to himself in an indivisible personal way. God freely
completes this creation with the free gift of himself in the
person of his Son. By this act of sovereign divine benevolence
he defines with utmost clarity the fantastic destiny for which
he meant man from the beginning. The incarnate
Son is God himself revealed in the world as Son of the
Father, Son of Mary, Son of Adam. The man Jesus Christ
shows is man in a personal oneness of life with God; he is
the new Adam, *the Man, the first-born of all creation* (*Col.* 1:15),
the first-born among many brothers (*Rom.* 8:29).

The Constitution on the Church in the Modern World
expresses this:

Only in the mystery of the incarnate Word does the
mystery of man take on light. For Adam, the first man,
was a figure of him who was to come, namely Christ the
Lord. Christ, the final Adam, by the revelation of the
mystery of the Father and his love, fully reveals man to
himself and makes his supreme calling clear . . . He who
is 'the image of the invisible God' (*Col.* 1:15) is himself the
perfect man (Par. 22).

These ideas on the primacy of Christ which have been
given their most forceful expression in our day by the great
Protestant theologian Karl Barth, are associated in our own
theological tradition with the Scotist school. One of the
most typical theses of the Scotists was that even if Adam
had not sinned Christ would nonetheless have become man.
Such a thesis must however remain in the realm of the
hypothetical, for concretely and historically we know man
sinned. Our records of the revelation of God's beneficent
activity towards man start from this fact. The written
revelation tells us in its very first pages of man's sin and

God's reaction. The divine interventions on behalf of man
of which revelation tells us are all redemptive in character
directed as they are to man already in a sinful situation.
God's love reveals itself because of man's situation as love
for the sinner. It is a saving love. The wonderful divine
plan of God to unite all men with himself in a personal
union of love is qualified already from the start by the fact
of man's sin.

God made man free. The records of revelation assure us
that man, made good by God, turned himself towards evil
and away from God. The history of God's dealings with
man which is written down in the books of the Old Testament
from Genesis onward, is an account of God's fidelity and
man's recurring faithlessness relieved by occasional fitful
spells of faithfulness. The history of Israel is a reproduction
on a smaller scale of world history. Even God's chosen
people creates a sinful history. We are not then surprised if
the universal story of man is the story of accumulation of
sin on sin. We are not amazed at St Paul's scorching words
in his epistle to the Romans, for the universal experience of
man testifies to their truth:

What can be known of God is plain to man because God
has shown it to him ever since the creation of the world –
his invisible nature, eternal power and deity have been
clearly perceived in the things that were made. So they
are without excuse, for although they knew God they did
not honour him as God or give thanks to him, but became
futile in their seeking and their empty minds were
darkened, and claiming to be wise they became fools and
exchanged the glory of the immortal God for images
resembling mortal man or birds, or animals or reptiles.
And therefore God gave them up in the lust of their hearts
to impurity and to the dishonouring of their bodies
among themselves because they exchanged the truth about
God for lies and worshipped and served the creature
rather than the creator (*Rom.* 1:19 ff.).

The history of humanity is then a history of sin and as generation follows generation the burden of sin grows, the world becomes a world of sin, and man, a creature destined to be taken up into God as sharer in the sonship of Christ, finds himself alone. He is alienated from God, not only that, he is divided from his fellow-man. Raising himself up against God he finds that in doing this he cuts himself off not only from God but from his fellow-men too. The Tower of Babel story in the book of Genesis brings this out well. Man the sinner, however, is not only at odds with his fellow-man and a rebel against God, but he is also divided in himself, finding elements of conflict in his own being. This point emerges clearly in the other account of the Fall in the first chapters of Genesis.

Christ, the Redeemer

It was into this sin-filled world, to live within its sinful history, that God sent his Son in the incarnation. The Son of God in becoming man took to himself a human race which was a fallen race. Though himself personally sinless he had to live out his life on this earth as one of sinful humanity. This is a most basic point to which we must return again and again. If we are not to give the impression in our theology of the redemption that the saving work of God the Son is some kind of detached divine activity in which God for appearance's sake acts like a man, we must emphasize again and again the reality and the depth of the involvement in the sinful condition of man which the incarnation means. Any tendency in our thinking and talking about the incarnation and the redemption which reduces the reality of God's coming in sinful flesh must be strenuously resisted because it runs counter to the clear testimony of Scripture. It is necessary to be on our guard against what we might call a kind of Monophysite over-emphasis on the divinity of Christ at the expense of his humanity, for this reduces the human reality of his earthly existence and makes it into some kind of special life, not really lived in the conditions

of this world. It may have been just this danger of under-
valuing the human in the incarnation which was in the
mind of the apostle John, the herald of the divine Logos
when he wrote, not that the Word was made man, but that
'the Word was made flesh and lived amongst us' (*John* 1:14).
I point out our not taking the human in the incarnation
seriously enough, as something to be avoided, because I
believe that this has been a weakness in our Catholic
manuals of Christology, and indeed in our Christology in
general. It may be that liberal Protestantism culminated in
setting before us a purely human Christ, but I think that we
must ask ourselves now if our effort to oppose this has not
taken us too far in the opposite direction. It is beyond
question that the Christ presented in our dogmatic tracts
possesses a true humanity, but it seems to me to be a
humanity of an order somewhat other than that which the
Christ of the Scriptures has. See, for example, what the
textbooks make of the Gospel phrase '*Eloi, Eloi, lama
sabachthani:* My God, my God, why has thou forsaken me'
(*Mark* 15:34) or what they make of some of the Christological
statements from the epistle to the Hebrews:

In the days of his flesh Jesus offered up prayers and
supplications with loud cries and tears to him who was
able to save him from death and he was heard for his
godly fear. Although he was a Son he learned obedience
through what he suffered and being made perfect he
became the source of eternal salvation to all who obey
him, being designated by God a high priest after the
order of Melchizedek (*Heb.* 5:7-10) . . . For we have not
a high priest who is unable to sympathise with our weak-
nesses but one who in every respect has been tempted as
we are, yet without sinning (*Heb.* 4:15).

If our Christology and Soteriology minimises Christ's
humanness, and his involvement, his solidarity with us
sinners, then it needs to be recalled to biblical statements

such as we find in the second chapter of Paul's epistle to the Philippians where we read: 'He emptied himself taking the form of a servant and being born in the likeness of man'. And we find in the second epistle to the Corinthians the even more astounding sentence: 'For our sake God made him to be sin, who knew no sin' (2 *Cor.* 5:21).

Christ entered really into our human condition. He is truly the Lamb of God who bears the sins of the world. The great Johannine exposition of his passage to the Father underlines the reality of his oneness with sinful man as does the Pauline contrast of the earthly servant and the enthroned Lord. The passage of the Son from the world of death and darkness to the world of light and life, to his Father's glory, is a real passage. The humiliation of the servant is a real humiliation, a real *kenosis*. It is not just a pretence, a hiding of glory for our edification. The Son of God in no way ceases to be God, but he does assume humanity which is linked to Adam, that is to say, fallen humanity.

The coming in the flesh of the Son of God brings to pass a mysterious situation in which the all-holy and all-glorious Son of God is made less than the Father, achieves a certain distance from his Father, accepts solidarity with us sinners and a certain being-away-from his Father. In fact if the word would not be misunderstood one could speak of a certain alienation, a certain depth of darkness which Christ endured which is nowhere so strikingly expressed as in St Mark's astonishingly audacious phrase which he reports on the lips of the dying Christ: 'My God, my God, why hast thou forsaken me?' (cf. *Ps.* 22:2). We are touching here on the inner mysteries of Christ's being, on the depths below depths which the incarnation of the only-begotten Son of God into the sinful race of Adam involves.

Christ comes in the likeness of sinful flesh – likened to us in *all* things, sin alone excepted as St Paul tells us (*Heb.* 4:15). He becomes subject to death and suffering – those things which are the outward signs of the sinfulness of the sons of Adam. He is tempted in every respect as we are, yet he does

not sin. He is 'for a little while' made lower than the angels
(*Heb.* 2:9.). In his earthly condition he possesses the Spirit
in abundance as the stories of his baptism seek to bring out
(*Mark* 1:9–11, *John* 1:29–34, *Matt.* 3:13–17 and *Luke*
3:21–22) but the Spirit does not yet fully possess and
penetrate his created nature. Thus he prays to the Father on
the eve of his suffering in the last days of his earthly existence:
'Father, glorify thy Son' (*John* 17:1). 'The Spirit was not
given because Jesus was not yet glorified' (*John* 7:39) St John
writes. The redemptive work of Christ as described in
Scripture shows him working his way from a freely accepted
unglorified human situation of mysterious and profound
solidarity with sinners to the glory which is rightfully his
as the Son of God. In his incarnation the Son accepts as the
starting-point of his redemptive ascent to the Father a
oneness with sinners which is rightly described as a being-
away-from the Father. This is a deeply mysterious fact we
have perhaps not sufficiently emphasized.

Sin is ultimately the reason for God's Son having to
assume an *unglorified nature*. Sin marked the world into which
he came 'for all have sinned and fall short of the glory of
God' (*Rom.* 3:23). Sin marked even the personal existence
of Christ in that it seems to have been able to divide him
from his Father, even if he was personally sinless. As
Schillebeeckx expresses it:

There is a sense in which the earthly Christ is not 'with
the Father' no matter how closely he, as man too, may be
united to the Father in loving attachment. This is not
a question of some kind of local separation that supposedly
would be involved in Christ's being on earth while the
Father is 'in heaven'. But still it does mean some kind of
'absence from home' or 'estrangement' from God. For
'while we are at home in the body (the actual meaning
is while we are men existing in the fallen state) we are
away from the Lord' (2 *Cor.* 5:6). (*Christ, the Sacrament*,
Sheed & Ward, London 1963, p. 29.)

The redemption is not one single divine act essentially
unrelated to the rest of Christ's history. Neither is the
incarnation a temporal assumption of human nature *qua*
nature. The incarnation means being man, within the conditions of time and space; it means living a historical existence
in freedom. It necessarily implies in Christ a growth, a
development.

No man is born a complete man. He is born to achieve
the fulness of manhood in the exercise of responsible freedom.
He is made in such a way, given existence in such a world
that he is invited to make himself, to collaborate in freedom
with his maker.

Christ grew to the fulness of manhood and this growing
to the fulness of manhood which is implied in the incarnation
itself was also a growing towards the fulness of his status as
Christ the Redeemer, the Lord.

The redemption is a process, a movement, a series of
historical events with a supra-temporal meaning and
effectiveness; it is the *mysteries of Christ's flesh* to use St
Thomas's expression. The incarnation is not the assumption
of human nature and no more; it is the assumption of a
personal human destiny and history which is redemptive.
And it is only when Christ's personal human history is
complete and, having passed through the events of his life,
death and resurrection, he sits at the right hand of God
sending the Spirit that man, in the humanity of Christ, has
entered into the glory of the Lord which is what redemption
means.

Christ becomes the Redeemer. The incarnation grows
towards its final realization in the exaltation of Jesus. The
exaltation of Jesus as the Lord is the incarnation of the
Son fulfilled and the redemption is the process of this
fulfilment.

Thus even if he was personally sinless, Christ, having
assumed the humanity of sin, had laboriously to work his way
back to the Father along the path marked out for him by
his Father's will.

The Obedience of the Son

The life of Christ on earth was a life of obedience to his Father's will. His life among men was summed up in the expression: 'I always do what is pleasing to him' (*John* 8:29). He was the beloved Son whose 'food was to do the will of him who sent me' (*John* 4:34). He went from the Father into a world, into a humanity alienated from God to bear witness to the Father, to be obedient. This obedience of the Son extended even to the giving up of his human life in testimony to his Father. This was the supreme point of the Son's abasement, the supreme expression of divine and human love, for the Father gave his only-begotten Son over to death for us, and the Son laid down his life for his friends. The redemption is best understood as the living out in human terms of the life of perfect sonship. It was this living out of perfect sonship in an alienated world which brought Christ to the cross. With Christ's death on the cross the divine redemptive activity reached its pivotal point. To the utter self-abasement of the Son which revealed and gave testimony to the Father, the only God, there corresponded a revelation of the Son in the fulness of his glory, which was the correlative of the cross. This was the resurrection, the raising to God's right hand. The Father glorified his Son, bringing him out of the world of sin and death to the conditions of which he had submitted himself without reserve; and made him enter on a new existence, enter a new world where his existence, his humanity were completely penetrated with the Spirit and in which he himself stands as the Lord of creation and the giver of the Spirit to his brethren.

The redemption is effected in the transformation of the manhood of Christ, in its complete taking over by the Spirit. In Christ's humanity Adam is established first in the new condition of man – life in the Spirit. From the lowliness, abasement and solidarity with fallen mankind in their sinfulness which he freely chose, Christ is brought to the glory of God's right hand. Through the suffering and death which he had endured as the obedient servant and in direct correlation with that suffering and death Jesus is made Lord, raised from the dead. Henceforth he lives, and gives life to all who accept him as the Lord. This is the way that Scripture presents the doctrine of the redemption. Christ has revealed in his own life, death and resurrection, the meaning of sin and the meaning of love. God has shown us in the mysteries of Christ's flesh that the Father, Son and holy Spirit love us with a love that overcomes our sinfulness.

Sin and Repentance:
From Alienation to Wholeness

DENIS O'CALLAGHAN

The Christian life, in its most real and personal terms, is man's entry into the community of love and knowledge which unites Father, Son and holy Ghost in the Trinity. This is the meaning of grace. Baptism introduces the child into the life of the Trinity, but this relationship, real as it is, is as yet unconscious and unexpressed on his part. In the adult, grace calls for communication, for the actual knowledge and love of God. Otherwise an adult relationship would not be fully realized. In this knowledge and love the Christian on earth has already a foretaste of the heaven which seals the God-man relationship in fulfilment and in eternity; grace is glory in exile, glory is grace at home. But during his probationary period the Christian works out his way to God amid human weakness and uncertainty. He is limited in his knowledge of God – he sees, but not clearly: 'For now we see in a mirror dimly, but then face to face. Now I know in part; then I shall understand fully, even as I have been fully understood.'[1] He is unfaithful in his love of God – he responds to God's invitation, but not always promptly and unfailingly. 'If we say we have no sin, we deceive ourselves, and the truth is not in us.'[2]

---

[1] *1 Cor.* 13:12.
[2] *1 John* 1:8.

Sin is the occupational hazard of the Christian on earth. But it is consoling to know that even though it turns man from God it does not turn God from man. God's love is ready to forgive when the sinner returns: 'If we confess our sins, he is faithful and just, and will forgive our sins and cleanse us from all unrighteousness.'[3]

Sin and repentance are then closely related ideas; the fact of sin explains the need for repentance, the nature of sin determines the pattern of repentance. Before we come to analyse the nature of sin or repentance, we must examine certain factors which are presupposed in their description and very nature, namely, man's freedom and his awareness of God.

Man is created in freedom. Of all God's earthly creatures he is given the power to turn away from God. Lord of his destiny he may deny the very purpose of his creation. This is the awesome responsibility which makes the human being what he is. Again, man is called to grace in freedom. He may refuse the invitation of Christ, *Come follow me*, or he may accept at first and later abandon it, his love 'like a morning cloud that goes early away.'[4] The parable of the sower teaches that the offer of the kingdom of heaven respects man's freedom, even to the point of allowing him to damn himself in refusal.

The mystery of sin is fundamentally the mystery of human freedom. If one refuses to admit freedom then one has emptied sin of its real meaning, that of culpability or of guilt. Guilt means a wrong situation for which the sinner is directly responsible. Without freedom one would see man as more acted upon than acting, a creature of circumstances, conditioned by the ebb and flow of bio-physical and social influences.

True, human action does not take place in a vacuum. It is situated historically as the act of this individual in the context of the here and now. We admit that sometimes what

---

[3] *1 John* 1:9.
[4] *Hos.* 6:4.

appears to be sin is simply the activity of a diseased personality, we admit that man is ordinarily subject to inner and external pressures, (psychological, social, etc.) which lessen his freedom, but we state that the normal man is generally responsible or personally answerable for his actions. To say otherwise would be to deprive man of his God-like glory as person, and to wipe out at a single stroke not only blame for failure but credit for success. Man is aware of an 'ought' or 'ought not' within himself. The guilt feelings which generally follow on sin are not neurotic or instinctive reflexes. They are the reactions of intelligent conscience in appreciation of a real situation of guilt.

Awareness of God is presupposed in genuine sin. The humanist may speak of sin and repentance, he may have a very real sense of sin and repentance, but he does not appreciate their full meaning. For him sin may be a fault or defect by which man fails himself, by which he falls short of his standards, or by which he injures the dignity or exploits the position of another person. Repentance may be the sense of remorse which leads him to renew his allegiance to his philosophy of life, or the acceptance of responsibility for the injury he has done the other, and the consequent effort to repair it. Sin and repentance are all these things, but this is not the whole story. A true sense of sin and repentance presupposes a true sense of God. From this point of view it may be said that only the saint has a true sense of sin.

In the Old Testament one can see a gradual growth in the understanding of individual responsibility and personal guilt. The question was naturally confused by the carry-over from primitive times and from less enlightened neighbours of notions of sin based on taboo, superstition or ritual impurity.[5] God could be regarded as punishing with death the sin of Uzzah, who simply laid a hand on the ark to steady it over a rocky patch of ground.[6] The same kind of

---

[5] *Ezek.* 18:5-9.
[6] 1 *Chron.* 13:9.

material sacrilege is said to be punished by death in the case
of the inexperienced sons of Aaron, who offered sacrifice
without observing the proper rubrics of the ceremony.[7]
Then again the idea of sin was confused in the concept of
corporate responsibility, by which the nation or family was
regarded as guilty of the sin of one of its members.[8] Still, the
biblical idea of sin as a deliberate personal offence against
God gradually emerged. The sin of Adam and Eve and the
lust of David for Bathsheba are presented as quite deliberate
in that the sinner was tempted and, having considered the
situation, decided to surrender. The principle of personal
responsibility is taught in such texts as:

> What do you mean by repeating this proverb concerning
> the land of Israel: The fathers have eaten sour grapes and
> the children's teeth are set on edge. As I live, says the
> Lord God, this proverb shall no more be used by you in
> Israel. Behold, all souls are mine; the soul of the father
> as well as the soul of the son is mine: the soul that sins
> shall die . . . The son shall not suffer for the iniquity of
> the father, nor the father suffer for the iniquity of the son.
> The righteousness of the righteous shall be upon him-
> self, and the wickedness of the wicked shall be upon
> himself. [9]

Finally, sin was conceived as an offence against God in that
it constituted disobedience to the authority of the supreme
Lord of creation, in that it was disloyalty to the Lord of the
Covenant, and in that it was ingratitude to a loving Father
and Spouse. The prophets were particularly insistent on
these latter aspects: 'I thought you would call me, my
Father, and would not turn from following me. Surely, as
a faithless wife leaves her husband, so you have been
faithless to me, O house of Israel.'[10] 'Hear, O heavens, and
give ear O earth; for the Lord has spoken. Sons have I

---

[7] *Num.* 3:4.
[8] 2 *Sam.* 12:10; 21:1; 24:15; cf. *John* 9:2.
[9] *Ezek.* 18:2-20.
[10] *Jer.* 3:19-20.

reared and brought up, but they rebelled against me. The ox knows its owner, and the ass its master's crib; but Israel does not know, my people does not understand.'[11]

The New Testament brought special emphasis to the concept of God as a loving Father, and of sin as a betrayal of this love. The depth of God's love and the enormity of sin are preached in most concrete fashion in the advent and passion of Christ: 'In this the love of God was made manifest among us, that God sent his only Son into the world, so that we might live through him. In this is love, not that we loved God, but that he loved us and sent his Son to be the expiation for our sins.'[12] The mission of Christ was a mission of redemption, a mission to heal sin in all its forms. Even when he healed bodily infirmity he reminded his hearers that sin was the disease which was the root of the evil. To the paralytic at the Sheep Gate he said: 'Sin no more, that nothing worse befall you.'[13] To the paralytic let down through the roof Jesus said: 'My son, your sins are forgiven.'[14] In the Passion Christ made common cause with sinners and in the course of this he teaches us the chasm which sin places between God and man. 'All we like sheep have gone astray, everyone has turned into his own way, and the Lord has laid on him the iniquity of us all.'[15] 'And about the ninth hour Jesus cried with a loud voice, 'My God, my God, why hast thou forsaken me?'[16]

Sin

In the analysis of the theological notion of sin three things claim attention – sin is alienation from God, it is a dividing factor in the community, and it disintegrates the person.

Sin alienates from God in that it is refusal to obey him as

[11]*Is.* 1:2-3.
[12]1 *John* 4:9-10.
[13]*John* 5:14.
[14]*Mark* 2:5.
[15]*Is.* 53:6-8.
[16]*Matt.* 27:46.

E

Creator and a refusal to love him as Father. It is man's 'I
will not serve' to the God who created him and who holds
him in the protection of his providence. It disturbs the
Creator-creature relation. Sin as disobedience is a description
which may appeal to a primitive people or to an immature
personality. It is, in its way, a valid definition, but it does
not plumb the depths of sin and will easily decline into
legalism and concentration on externals. Appreciating sin as
a refusal to love gives a far deeper insight into its real nature.
It is the Christian's 'I will not love' directed to the Father
who has loved him to the point of giving him a share in his
own life and of sending his Son to communicate to him this
life and love. Here sin is a break in the Father-son relationship. 'See what love the Father has given us, that we should
be called children of God; and so we are. . . No-one born of
God commits sin; for God's nature abides in him, and he
cannot sin because he is born of God.'[17] This is certainly the
idea of sin taught by Christ: God loved us and asks man's
love in return. Sin is the refusal to respond to God's
invitation.

Sin also divides man from man. It is *the* subversive force
in the community in that it poisons its general atmosphere
and introduces division and decay into it. Historically this
is the result of original sin. The happy relationship which
should unite God and man as also man and man has given
way to an uneasy co-existence marked by jealousy and
suspicion.

All men both Jews and Greeks are under the power of
sin, as it is written: 'None is righteous, no, not one; no-one
understands, no-one seeks for God, all have turned aside,
together they have gone wrong; no-one does good, not
even one. Their throat is an open grave, they use their
tongues to deceive. The venom of asps is under their lips.
Their mouth is full of curses and bitterness. Their feet
are swift to shed blood, in their paths are ruin and misery,

[17] I *John* 3:1-9.

and the way of peace they do not know. There is no fear
of God before their eyes.'[18]

It is obvious that some sins directly harm society, in that
they exploit or injure some individual member or society at
large. But every sin, no matter how secret and private, is a
divisive force in the community of charity in that it introduces disorder into some person's heart, with the result that
the community has in him a defective member. As St John
repeats in his epistles, the love-relationship with God is
inseparable from the love-relationship with fellow man. He
teaches us that the purpose of Christ's death was to draw
men together into a community of one mind, to unite into
one the children of God who were scattered abroad by sin.[19]

Finally sin disintegrates the sinner. It disorientates man
from the poles which give direction to his life, the love of God
and the love of his neighbour in God. His life becomes
centred on self or on selfish attachment to some creature.
Restlessness, dissipation and emptiness are the price of
violated conscience. Still, these may well be graces in
disguise to prompt the sinner to return to his Father's house.
The parable of the Prodigal Son teaches the value of the
grace of an uneasy conscience. In real perversity the voice of
conscience may be completely silenced so that man no longer
feels a need to live up to any moral standards. Here one is
dealing with a pathological disturbance of the human person.
Moral inertia is just as radical a disorder in the area of human
action as insanity is in the area of human intelligence.

The three elements of sin – alienation from God, division
among men, disintegration of the person – are properly
found in mortal sin. Originally the distinction between
mortal and venial sin was introduced in view of the
different consequences of these sins. Mortal sin is a total
break with God which is irreparable in the sense that when
sealed in death it merits exclusion from his sight for ever.

---

[18]*Rom.* 3:9-18.
[19]*John* 11:52.

That there exist essential differences in malice or guilt
between the sins which a man may commit is an indisputable
fact in scripture and tradition. St Paul lists certain sins which
exclude the sinner from 'the love of God' and from 'the
kingdom of God'.[20] It is in reference to these sins that one
reads: 'The wages of sin is death.'[21] As against this, Christ
directs his followers in the *Our Father* to pray for the forgiveness of their sins. There is question here of the daily weak-
nesses into which even the faithful lapse. 'We all make many
mistakes', says St James, and St John warns us: 'If we say
we have no sin we deceive ourselves, and the truth is not
in us.'[22]

The witness of the early Church holds strongly for the
distinction between light sin, which is expiated by prayer,
fasting and almsgiving, and grave sin, which excludes from
the Eucharist and requires submission to the penitential
discipline.[23] In earlier centuries the number of sins recognized
as grave in this way would have been few, and there was no
agreed catalogue of *peccata capitalia* or *mortalia* as distinct
from the *delicta leviora*. The additions to the central triad of
idolatry, murder and adultery depended to a large extent
on the traditions or circumstances of the various churches.
The detailed, but often arbitrary classifications of the
Penitentials, widely used in the seventh and eighth centuries,
prepared the way for the medieval *summae* or *manuales
confessariorum*. These in turn were the forerunners of our
institutiones morales. The care which these latter employ in
identifying mortal sin and in differentiating it from venial
sin is due in great part to the emphasis which Trent laid on
the need to confess all mortal sins by number and species.[24]

In medieval times some nominalists taught that the
distinction between mortal and venial sin, and between

---

[20]*Gal.* 5:19-20.
[21]*Rom.* 6:23.
[22]*James* 3:2; 1 *John* 1:8.
[23]Bernhard Poschmann, *Penance and the anointing of the sick*, London 1963,
24, 44-9.
[24]*Denz.* 899.

eternal and temporal punishment, was a purely extrinsic one imposed by a decree of God's sovereign will. On any real view of God's justice or providence this was inadmissible. Saner scholastic tradition accepted that God takes his human creatures seriously, and looked for the difference between the two kinds of sin in the kind of being man was and in the nature of his religio-moral activity. In general they traced the distinction between mortal and venial sin to the difference between acting directly against the law of God or the order of charity (*contra legem, contra caritatem*) and acting beyond or outside this law or order (*praeter legem, praeter caritatem*). For St Thomas mortal sin stands in direct opposition to man's last end (*inordinatio circa finem*), whereas venial sin affects the means (*inordinatio circa ea quae sunt ad finem*).[25] Of its nature mortal sin radically affects man's relation to God, it destroys the love of God in his heart, and makes something other than God his last end. Venial sin does not have the force to contradict man's direction to his last end, it is a slackening of pace and fervour but man still remains centred on God in love.[26]

It is true that in the assessment of the malice of his sin the sinner's disposition should be given a far greater place than it normally receives. The guilt of the person who falls after much conscience-stricken lying to himself about the nature or gravity of his sin must be seen in quite a different light from that of the man who sins with careless disregard for God's will. This would correspond to the biblical distinction between 'sins of weakness' and 'sins with hand upraised'. But to demand a total commitment to some sinful object with an express rejection of God would be to contradict the whole force of Christian tradition and the Bible itself. Christian tradition recognizes mortal sin not only in the rare case where there is an express intention of turning away from God, but also in the case where the sinner is led by selfish desire to choose something which he knows to be

[25]*S. theol.* 1a 2 ae, q. 88, art. 1.
[26]*S. theol.* 1a 2 ae, q. 88, art. 2.

seriously opposed to the will of God. This conscious turning
to the world (*conversio ad creaturam*) of its nature represents a
turning away from God (*aversio a Deo*), much though the
sinner regrets it.

The Bible distinguishes the 'sin unto death' mentioned in
St John's first epistle[27] from the more ordinary 'sins of
weakness' which exclude from the kingdom of heaven but
which can be expiated by repentance helped by the prayers
of the community. These latter include mortal sins in our
sense of the term even though they do not possess the
Satanic heinousness of the former. St John's 'sin unto death'
is the express rejection of the offer of salvation made by
God in Christ. This is equivalent to the sin against the light,
to 'the blasphemy against the holy Spirit' which the
Synoptics regard as unforgivable, as 'eternal sin'.[28] A man
in this state of final impenitence, of total rejection of God, is,
in St John's terrifying description, even beyond the reach
of the community's prayers. It is obvious that this is a rare
case, but there are frequent warnings in the New Testament
writings about the danger of losing the life of Christ through
the weakness of the flesh and the distractions of the world.
It is in this latter area that we must find what is commonly
known as mortal sin.

The key to the difference between mortal and venial sin
is not to be discovered by concentrating on the quality of the
sinner's personal decision to the exclusion of the external
object. To do so would be to ignore the fact that man is
incarnate in a body and is placed in the worldly order of
creation. Neither his spiritual decision nor his exterior
activity can provide a self-sufficient norm for human
activity. The choice of the will is embodied in the desire
or the performance of a definite course of action, and the

---

[27]'If anyone sees his brother committing a sin that is not unto death, he
will ask, and God will give him life for those whose sin is not unto death.
There is a sin which is unto death; I do not say that one should pray for that.
All wrongdoing is sin, but there is a sin which is not unto death.' (1 *John*
5:16-17.)

[28]*Matt.* 12:31-32; *Mark* 3:28-29; *Luke* 12:10.

moral judgement on rightness and wrongness must take both aspects into account.[29]

It seems that as between mortal and venial sin there is a fundamental distinction both in the quality of the free decision and in the extent of the matter involved. Every mortal sin implies a rejection of God. Granted that the rejection has not the absolute finality of St John's 'sin unto death', it is a provisional rejection in that it initiates a state which will exclude a man irrevocably from God if and when it is sealed in impenitent death. In mortal sin there is a fundamental choice in which a person's direction to his ultimate end is at stake. It is a radical orientation of the person in that the sinner fully engages himself and consciously commits himself to something which he knows to be directly opposed to the will of God. In venial sin man's total power of decision for evil is not involved. Since the issue at stake is not really significant in the order of the love of God or of neighbour, the moral decision takes place at a superficial or peripheral level. The *conversio ad creaturam* in mortal sin implies an *aversio a Deo* in that it effectively excludes God and destroys the direction to the last end – the final realization of this option is hell. The *conversio ad creaturam* in venial sin does not destroy the basic project of the love of God in the will of the sinner, even though it does involve a cooling or slackening in that love.

It appears that even the very quality of the decision involved suggests a difference in matter between mortal and venial sin. In mortal sin the object of decision is a serious violation of the moral order, it destroys some essential condition for the love of God, it attacks vital factors in man's relations with God and with the community, it cannot co-exist with charity. In venial sin the object is of marginal or secondary importance in the moral order. It is not the

---

[29]Most modern authors think along these lines. See Bernhard Haring, *The Law of Christ I*, Cork 1961, pp. 356-63; Piet Schoonenberg, *Man and Sin*, London 1965, 25-40; Louis Monden, *Sin, Liberty and the Law*, London 1966, 34-40.

kind of thing which radically disturbs man's relations with
God or with the community. Even when the sinner commits
this kind of sin with complete deliberation it does not, and
he knows that it does not, effect here and now a break with
God. This is simply accommodating oneself to the external
order of created reality in which human morality operates
and taking seriously the hierarchy of moral values within
this order. The relationship of human love provides some
analogy in its gradations from coolness for minor offences
to total rupture for grave faults.

At the same time if a person of satanic disposition clearly
and deliberately chooses to do something *because* it is a sin, if
he chooses to do it as a sign of his scorn for God's law and his
rebellion against God, this amounts to a rejection of God's
love not because of what he actually did (this may be quite
slight) but because of what it signified. In the wider context
it is hardly necessary to add that deliberate venial sin
disposes and prepares the sinner for mortal sin in that its
influence, peripheral as it may be, will gradually and
inevitably erode the centre of his moral being. Perhaps this
is the real malice of venial sin, that it constructs a slipway
which will launch one into mortal sin.

It is obvious that one cannot equate mortal sin with what
the moral and legal tradition call grave matter. To do so
would be to confuse two quite distinct orders of morality,
the objective and the subjective, law and conscience. It
would also be to ignore the very human and fallible influences
which have led to the recognition of some matter as grave
and other matter as light. Mortal sin is a complex reality.
It incorporates so many factors of individual and situation
that one should be very chary in giving judgement. Only
God can judge the malice of sin, and in the last analysis the
sinner must be left to his judgement and mercy.

Repentance

The call to repentance echoes throughout the Scriptures
from the prophets' 'Return to the Lord your God', through

John the Baptist's 'Do penance for the kingdom of heaven
is at hand', to Christ's 'Unless you repent, you will all
likewise perish', and the apostles' 'Repent and believe the
Gospel'. The New Testament uses a technical term,
metanoiein, to signify repentance. In its root meaning this
term underlines the change of heart which repentance
implies. The Old Testament had no such specialized term.
It employed the everyday words, especially the verb *shub*,
'to return'. This is a descriptive and dynamic term. It
suggests that as man freely left his God in sin he returns to
him freely in repentance. The prophets emphasize that in
this repentance God takes the initiative. In his mercy he
never forgets the sinner: 'Can a woman forget her suckling
child, that she should have no compassion on the son of her
womb? Even these may forget, yet I will not forget you.'[30]
'Behold I, I myself will search for my sheep, and will seek
them out. As a shepherd seeks out his flock when some of
his sheep have been scattered abroad, so will I seek out my
sheep; and I will rescue them from all places where they
have been scattered on a day of clouds and thick darkness. . . .
I will seek the lost, and I will bring back the strayed, and I
will bind up the crippled.'[31]

In the Old Testament we find some examples of penitential
liturgy (the pouring out of water before the Lord in 1 *Sam.*
7:6, the sending of the scapegoat into the wilderness in *Lev.*
16:20–23), and of penitential practices (the common usage
of fasting in sack-cloth and ashes), but we are frequently
reminded that external ceremonies and actions are of no
value in themselves. Genuine penance implies a change in
one's way of life and real sorrow for sin: 'Wash yourselves;
make yourselves clean . . . cease to do evil, learn to do
good';[32] 'circumcise your hearts. Wash your heart from
wickedness';[33] 'return to me with all your heart . . . rend

---

[30]*Is.* 49:15.
[31]*Ezek.* 34:11-16.
[32]*Is.* 1:16.
[33]*Jer.* 4:4-14.

your hearts and not your garments'.[34] The call 'turn now
every one of you from his evilways' is repeated time and
time again in Jeremiah.[35] Finally, it is taught by Ezekiel
that even though genuine penance guarantees God's
forgiveness it does not mean that the converted cannot fall
away again.

If a wicked man turns away from all his sins which he
has committed and keeps all my statutes and does what
is lawful and right, he shall surely live; he shall not die.
None of the transgressions which he has committed shall
be remembered against him; for the righteousness which
he has done he shall live. Have I any pleasure in the death
of the wicked, says the Lord God, and not rather that he
should turn from his way and live? But when a righteous
man turns away from his righteousness and commits iniquity
and does the same abominable things that the wicked man
does, shall he live? None of the righteous deeds which he
has done shall be remembered; for the treachery of which
he is guilty and the sin he has committed, he shall die.[36]

These same themes of penance are repeated for us in the
more familiar texts of the New Testament. Here God takes
the initiative in reconciling man to himself in the mystery
of love which is the incarnation and passion of his son.[37]
Again and again we are assured that we have forgiveness of
sin through Christ: 'My little children, I am writing this to
you that you may not sin; but if anyone does sin, we have an
advocate with the Father, Jesus Christ the righteous; and
he is the expiation for our sins, and not for ours only but for
the sins of the whole world.'[38] The good shepherd leaves the
ninety-nine sheep in the hills and goes out to search for the
single one that is lost and returns with it joyfully. The moral
which Jesus draws is: 'There will be more joy in heaven over

---

[34] *Joel* 2:12-13.
[35] e.g. *Jer.* 18:11; 25:5; 26:3, etc.
[36] *Ezek.* 18:21-24.
[37] Cf. 2 *Cor.* 5:19; 1 *John* 4:9-10.
[38] 1 *John* 2:1-2.

one sinner who repents than over ninety-nine righteous persons who need no repentance.'[39] We see this attitude of merciful forgiveness in Christ's dealing with the Magdalen, 'her sins which are many, are forgiven, for she loved much ... your faith has saved you; go in peace';[40] and with the woman convicted of adultery: 'Neither do I condemn you; go, and do not sin again.'[41] The whole theology of penance as the return of the sinner and as God's loving forgiveness is expressed most strikingly in the parable of the Prodigal Son.[42]

We have already said that the nature of sin determines the pattern of repentance. Repentance, therefore, counteracts or neutralizes the three destructive forces in sin. It is a conversion to God, a reconciliation with the community, and a reintegration of the person.

The conversion to God is summed up in the word contrition. This is nothing else than the faith, hope and charity of the sinner built on a humble acknowledgement of guilt. Humility is the primary and basic attitude of the sinner: 'Father, I have sinned against heaven and before you; I am no longer worthy to be called your son.'[43] There is no forgiveness for the self-righteous who refuses to acknowledge his sin. This is the moral of the parable of the Pharisee and the Publican.[44] Unfortunately, familiarity can dull the impact of its message, as it can dull the force of Christ's comments on the hypocrites who feign penance but remain hardened in heart. The sorrow of which we speak here is not wounded self-respect, remorse, annoyance at having shown weakness, feeling mortified. This is but pride in disguise. Genuine sorrow is the humble admission by the sinner that he has selfishly betrayed a Father's love and is not worthy to be called a son.

---

[39]*Luke* 15:7.
[40]*Luke* 7:47-50.
[41]*John* 8:11.
[42]*Luke* 15:11-32.
[43]*Luke* 15:21.
[44]*Luke* 18:9-14.

Following on the basic attitude of humility, contrition is an act of faith, hope, and charity, with special reference to the sinner's state. He firmly believes in God's willingness and power to forgive sin (faith); he trusts in his mercy and confidently hopes for the grace of pardon (hope); he expresses his attachment to God and his sorrow that he has offended him (charity). Love of God is an ingredient in every true repentance. If the motive of one's sorrow for sin is simply that one wishes to save one's skin and avoid hell there is no contrition. Contrition is not selfish fear or interest; there must be appreciation of an offence against God. This does not mean that the fear of hell cannot be an element, and a very telling element, in contrition. It does mean that the mere unrelieved, servile fear of hell is not contrition.

Repentance also implies reconciliation with the community. The sinner returns to the people of God, to the fold of the Good Shepherd. God is encountered in and through his Church, the community of charity. *Extra ecclesiam nulla salus* is as true for penance as for baptism – and raises similar difficulties. If baptism is the sacrament of incorporation into God's people, penance is the sacrament of return. Everyone who performs a genuine repentance, be he Christian or non-Christian, is justified in and through the Church of Christ, the continuing sacrament of redemption from sin. The approach to the priest in the confessional may appear a very private affair, but it is the official act of return to God's people. Reconciliation with the people of God is the condition of reconciliation with God or, in theological language, it is the *res et sacramentum* of penance. This was the force of the *pax cum ecclesia* of the early Church, and it is the force of the absolution today.

Genuine repentance requires that the sinner make amends for the injury which his sin has caused to the community. This may demand on occasion restitution for damage caused to a neighbour's reputation or property, or reparation for insult or scandal. This restitution or reparation is a test

of the sincerity of repentance. In addition, real contrition
also implies that hate and unforgiving pride are dead in the
heart of the sinner. In the Our Father we make the frighten-
ing request: 'Forgive us our offences as we forgive them who
offend against us', and Christ's exegesis does not soften its
force: 'For if you forgive men their offences, your heavenly
Father also will forgive you; but if you do not forgive men
their offences, neither will your Father forgive your
offences.'[45] 'Peter said to him, "Lord, how often shall my
brother sin against me, and I forgive him? As many as
seven times?" Jesus said to him, "I do not say to you seven
times seven, but seventy times." '[46] The moral of the parable
of the Merciless Servant – he was forgiven his debt but was
later made to pay in full when he had revealed his ungenerous
nature – is, 'so also my heavenly Father will do to every
one of you, if you do not forgive your brother from your
heart.'[47] The whole theme is summed up succinctly by St
John: 'If anyone says, "I love God", and hates his brother,
he is a liar.'[48]

The third element in repentance is the personal reintegration of the sinner. The formal act of reconciliation with
God is but a first step in what must be a radical process of
conversion. As the habit and attitude of sin gradually
corrupts and disintegrates the whole man, so the process of
conversion purifies and integrates him. Even though man
has turned away from sin he is still aware of a retrograde
tendency in his heart, he is still aware of the occasions and
attractions to sin presented by the world about him. 'Put
to death therefore what is earthly in you; immorality,
impurity, passion, evil desire and covetousness.'[49] This
'putting to death' of sin is the continual effort to kill what is
selfish in one's heart and to make God the centre of ones'

[45]*Matt.* 6-14.
[46]*Matt.* 18:21-22.
[47]*Matt.* 18:35.
[48]1 *John* 4:20.
[49]*Col.* 3:5.

life. This process of conversion may be called mortification
or integration. The more usual term, mortification (*nekro-
sis*), is favoured by St Paul. It refers to the struggle between
the spirit and the flesh, the principle of new life and the still
unregenerate man. This latter must be neutralized. The
word integration emphasizes the more positive side of the
programme. It implies the mustering of all one's forces so
that one may direct and centre one's whole life on God.
It is inspired by the love of God and the desire to commit
oneself completely to him. This emphasis on integration
gives a real personal meaning to what is called 'the debt of
satisfaction for sin', and removes from it the suggestion of an
arbitrary fine imposed by a vindictive God. In great part,
then, satisfaction is simply the need for purification of heart,
for the correction of disordered tendencies in the sinner,
who has indulged himself selfishly and irresponsibly.

No matter how positive or optimistic theology may become
it must take account of sin. To ignore it, or to play it down,
would be to close one's eyes to the facts. But there is a
difference of approach in the attitude of the priest in the
pulpit and in that of the priest in the confessional. In the
pulpit he is called on to show man his sinfulness, to hold up a
mirror to his true state, to educate his conscience, and to call
him to repentance. This is his prophetic mission, and the
priest may not shirk it. Naturally he will not name names,
but he will show the same courage which Nathan showed
when he said to King David: 'You are the man, (described
in my parable)'[50] or which John the Baptist showed when he
said to King Herod: 'It is not lawful for you to have your
brother's wife.'[51] This task of calling on men to recognize
their sin is, in a way, more urgent today than ever before.
In the ages of faith sin was seen as sin; there may have been
sinners on the grand scale, but they were also penitents on
the grand scale. As Pius XII mentioned a decade ago, the
sin of contemporary society is that it has lost to a large

[50] *2 Sam.* 12:7.
[51] *Mark* 6:18.

extent the very sense of sin. The role of the priest in the confessional is different. Here he is called on to receive the sinner with the welcome and mercy which Christ showed. He must recognize the goodwill of the sinner as Christ did in the case of Zacchaeus: 'Today salvation has come to this house, for the Son of man came to seek and to save the lost.'[52] All in all the priest has the paradoxical task of discomforting the comfortable and comforting the discomfited.

---

[52]*Luke* 19:9-10.

The Church:
Community of Love

KEVIN MCNAMARA

God's plan in revealing himself is to unite all mankind to himself, to gather all into one. At the end of time, we are taught in the Conciliar Constitution *Lumen Gentium*, 'all just men from the time of Adam, "from Abel, the just one, to the last of the elect" will be gathered together with the Father in the universal Church.'[1] This is the 'mystery' or secret plan of God of which St Paul speaks in the epistle to the Ephesians:

> In him we have redemption through his blood, the forgiveness of our trespasses, according to the riches of his grace which he lavished upon us. For he has made known to us in all wisdom and insight the mystery of his will, according to his purpose which he set forth in Christ as a plan for the fulness of time, to unite all things in him, things in heaven and things on earth.[2]

The same teaching is expressed more concisely in the first epistle to Timothy:

> God our Saviour . . . desires all men to be saved and to come to the knowledge of the truth.[3]

---

[1]Art. 2.
[2]*Eph.* 1:7-10.
[3]1 *Tim.* 2:3f.

68

This design of God appears already in the biblical narrative concerning the call of the first man. Here, at the very outset of salvation history, we meet the idea of corporate personality which is destined to play so central a role in man's dealings with God as described in the Bible. Adam is not just an individual man; he is in some sense the entire human race. Given the opportunity to accept or decline God's friendship, his choice is the choice of all men. It was God's will that this choice should have been a positive one. In this way he would have already established the human race as his people and the knowledge of him would have been freely available to all.

The Corporate Vocation of Israel

Adam, however, rejected God's offer of a supernatural destiny. A new plan of salvation was therefore necessary, for God's will in regard to man remained unchanged. Again, this plan had for its object the human race as a whole, and it was entirely in keeping with its corporate and universal scope that God began his work of restoration by calling not individuals but an entire community. He disclosed himself first to the people of Israel and it was his design that this people should gradually expand until it embraced all mankind in a single great, holy people of God. We find this idea expressed, for example, by Isaiah, who visualizes Mount Sion, i.e. Jerusalem, as a centre of spiritual teaching for all mankind in the future:

> It shall come to pass in the latter days that the mountain of the house of the Lord shall be established as the highest of the mountains, and shall be raised above the hills; and all the nations shall flow to it, and many people shall come and say: 'Come, let us go up to the mountain of the Lord, to the house of the God of Jacob; that he may teach us his ways and that we may walk in his paths'.[4]

How was this to be accomplished? Only through Christ,

---

[4] *Is.* 2:2f.

F

the New Adam, the one appointed by God to be the man
for all men, to sum up all mankind in himself. Through
Christ, not only the Israelites, of whom he was one by birth,
but all men, could receive salvation. Christ therefore is the
point at which Israel breaks down the barriers which had
confined God's holy people within the limits of a single
nation, and opens out to embrace mankind as a whole. At the
same time Christ represents the pinnacle of Israel's religious
development. Despite its repeated infidelities and, in the face
of every new advance by God, its corporate failure to live a
life worthy of its calling, God was nevertheless achieving his
purpose. He preserved for himself, as the Bible puts it, a
'holy remnant', a little group of devout and holy people
from among whom, at the summit of their spiritual development, the Messiah would arise. In Jesus Christ all that had
gone before reaches its fulfilment, but in a way that immeasurably surpasses anything already achieved. In Christ
men can attain real and lasting intimacy with God.
For he is the Son, the true, eternal Son who knows the
Father perfectly and who has come to disclose him as he is.
From Christ flows the life of grace, of fellowship with the
Father in knowledge and love. It is in this fellowship,
essentially, that the Church consists. The Church is the
world-wide community of those who, entering into the
inheritance of Israel, possess in Christ divine friendship and
share in Christ's knowledge of the Father.

The formation of this community is the end God has in
view in all his dealings with Israel. That is why the call he
addresses to Israel is a community call, a call extended to,
and creating, a corporate people. Revelation, we have seen,
is God disclosing himself to men in order to enter into
fellowship with them. He invites men to yield themselves
freely to the advances of divine love, thereby breaking out of
their own isolation and selfishness. In so far as they respond
to this invitation, they are radically transformed and raised
up to share in the life of God himself, a life of complete
and unlimited self-giving.

In this light, the entire scope of God's plan for Israel may be summed up under two headings: God makes himself known as the God of infinite love, and, in the process of so doing, he gradually fashions Israel after his own likeness. In one complex process God both reveals the pattern to which Israel is to be conformed and actually shapes Israel to this design. It is here that the significance of God's calling of a people, and not merely of individuals, clearly emerges. It is not enough that the individual should seek to give himself to God; he must also seek to give himself to his fellows. Or, rather, it is only in giving himself to his fellows that he can fully meet the demand to yield himself to God. For, like himself, his fellows too are being made after God's image. God, in other words, appears before him in the persons of his brethren, and maintaining a loving and harmonious relationship with them is an essential part of the response of love which God demands of him.

It is against this background that God's dealings with Israel through the intermediacy of the Law are to be understood. The Law arises from the covenant, which forms the basis of the new relationship between God and Israel. This covenant God establishes with the people as a whole; indeed, it is precisely to the covenant that Israel owes its existence as a people. We see this clearly from the account of the formation of the covenant in the book of Exodus:

And Moses went up to God and the Lord called him out of the mountain, saying: 'Thus you shall say to the house of Jacob and tell the people of Israel. You have seen what I did to the Egyptians and how I bore you on eagle's wings and brought you to myself. Now therefore if you will obey my voice and keep my covenant, you shall be my own possession among all peoples; for all the earth is mine, and you shall be to me a kingdom of priests and a holy nation'.[5]

The new relationship of Israel to Yahweh to which this

---

[5] *Exod.* 19:3-6.

covenant gives rise is expressed in the Law, which, like the
covenant itself, is a community affair. This is already
implied in the choice of special representatives, of whom
Moses is the prototype, to mediate the Law to others. It is
only within the framework of a community, which is
unified and bound together through the common link
of the members with God's selected spokesman, that access
to the Law is possible.

Further, the Law lays down norms of conduct for the
individual's relationship not only with God but also with his
brethren. Since God is a God of justice and truthfulness, a
God of love and compassion, these virtues must mark the
individual Israelite's relations with his fellow-Israelites.
The purpose of the second table of the Decalogue is to
define these community obligations, and the second great
precept of the Law, 'Thou shalt love thy neighbour as
thyself', sums them all up in terms of their basic meaning.
The various Commandments derive their significance from
the fact that they prescribe the conditions in which, in the
various spheres of life, the individual can express his love
for his fellows and thereby demonstrate his fidelity to the
demands made on him by the God of love. In its further
applications the Law unfolds into a comprehensive code of
religious, social and political rules: rules concerning the
appointment, duties and privileges of Israel's priests, the
relationship between masters and servants, marriage, the
ownership, sale and inheritance of property. These enact-
ments are evidently intended to preserve the social unity of
the Israelites and safeguard their distinct existence as a
people, free from contamination by other nations. When in
due course the prophets make their appearance in Israel,
their task is to continue what the Law has begun, to keep
alive Israel's self-consciousness as God's chosen people, and
to develop further the bonds uniting it to God and binding
it together as a single community.

All through the Old Testament the corporate character of
Israel's life and destiny is stressed. We find, for example,

that Israel as a whole is spoken of as God's son, as if the entire nation were but a single person: 'Israel is my son, my first-born.'[6] Indeed, the very name Israel by which the people is known is originally the name of an individual man, the father of the twelve patriarchs, also known as Jacob, who somehow embodies the entire nation. Further, Israel's kings, especially King David, embody in their person the whole people, whose destiny is inextricably linked to their personal histories and fortunes. It is above all in the writings of the prophet Isaiah, however, where we find the mysterious figure of the Servant of Yahweh, that this solidarity of Israel is expressed. The servant is at one and the same time an individual and a community. In Isaiah (41:8 ff.) it is the entire people that Yahweh addresses as his servant:

But you Israel, my servant, Jacob whom I have chosen, the offspring of Abraham my friend, you whom I took from the ends of the earth and called from its farthest corners, saying to you, 'you are my servant, I have chosen you and not cast you off', fear not for I am with you, be not dismayed for I am your God; I will strengthen you, I will help you, I will uphold you with my victorious right hand.

But in the following chapter (*Is.* 42:1 ff.) we find that the servant is an individual:

Behold my servant whom I uphold, my chosen in whom my soul delights. I have put my spirit upon him; he will bring forth justice to the nations. He will not cry or lift up his voice or make it heard in the street; a bruised reed he will not break and a dimly burning wick he will not quench; he will faithfully bring forth justice. He will not fail or be discouraged till he has established justice in the earth and the coast lands wait for his law.

---

[6] *Exod.* 4:22.

The servant, then, is both the entire Israelite people and a chosen individual who sums up the people in himself and offers himself as a sacrificial victim on its behalf. Indeed, he offers himself not only on behalf of Israel, as Isaiah brings out clearly later, but on behalf of the entire human race.

A Holy People

In return for the special favours he showed them, God looked for a fitting response from his people. This may be summed up under the heading of a holy life. 'Be ye holy, as I, the Lord your God, am holy'[7] – this is the fundamental and inescapable rule of life of the people whom God has chosen. Because this people was being fashioned after his image, his holiness was to be the model and goal of their corporate life. The holiness of God means that he is altogether different from mankind, a being above and beyond all that man can experience, accomplish or even conceive. God is not bound up with this world, nor does he in any way depend on it for his happiness. His life has its own eternal origins and follows its own sovereign rhythm, and nothing can be added or contributed to it from outside. God is God because he is entirely self-sufficient, the one who, in contrast to all creatures, possesses the absolute fulness of being and life and has no need to turn elsewhere for his own fulfilment. This was the idea to which Yahweh gave expression when he revealed to Israel that he was the Holy One, and which Israel, without having worked out a detailed understanding of it, nevertheless securely grasped in its essentials. The consequences too, Israel saw clearly: because its God was the Holy One, Israel itself was called to holiness, to a consecrated life. Israel's destiny was to keep itself free from the worship of false gods. It was obliged to be faithful to the one true God who had called it, to rely only on him, and to seek its happiness in exclusive dedication to, and fellowship with him.

The implications of this holiness of life to which Israel

---

[7]*Lev.* 11:45.

was called may be summed up under the headings of faith, hope and charity. Because of the future Messiah with whom they afforded a link, these virtues were possible for Israel. Through faith, Israel accepted in obedience, humility and fidelity the word of God, which was already an anticipation of the personal Word of God incarnate in Christ. It was therefore through faith in the coming Messiah that Israel achieved this initial degree of union with God.

Israel is also united to God by a steadfast hope. It relies on God to save it in all the dangers that threaten it. Again, however, it is in the coming of the Messiah, by which the joys of paradise will be restored, that this saving process will reach its climax. All the saving acts of God in the Old Testament are so many instalments and promises of the supreme and definitive saving act he will accomplish through the Messiah. In its hope no less than in its faith, Israel is already benefiting from the sanctifying role of the Messiah, who one day will establish the definitive covenant between mankind and God.

Lastly and principally, Israel is united to God by charity. Love of God above all things and brotherly love of the neighbour are the two great pillars of the law. The self-sacrificing love of the Servant of God who, in filial obedience to God, suffers and dies to save his people, is the model for all Israel, both community and individuals:

> Surely he has borne our griefs and carried our sorrows; yet we esteemed him stricken, smitten by God and afflicted. . . . By his knowledge shall the righteous one, my servant, make many to be accounted righteous, and he shall bear our iniquities. Therefore I will divide him a portion with the great and he shall divide the spoil with the strong; because he poured out his soul to death and was numbered with the transgressors; yet he bore the sin of many and made intercession for the transgressors.[8]

Once more, however, it is only in Christ, the true Servant,

---

[8] *Is.* 53:4, 11f.

that Israel actually rises to the heights of this vocation to love. In Christ, Israel gives a supreme expression of love of God and love of man, love of all men without exception. In so far as it achieved genuine love prior to the coming of the Messiah, – and despite its infidelities, it did achieve such love at least in some of its number – Israel was sharing in advance in this perfect exercise of love by the Messiah. Anticipating the charity of Christ in this way, in many of its members it rose to a high level of union with God. In this fellowship the holiness of life to which Israel was called, and which already existed through faith and hope, reached its highest point. Here, also, the unifying effects of a holy life among the Israelites themselves emerge most clearly: if they were already bound together by a common faith and a common hope, that is by their common adherence to a true – or faithful – and saving God, it was in charity that these bonds culminated and became most effective.

As far as the individual Israelite was concerned, the significance of Israel's corporate calling as God's holy people was quite clear. It was only on condition of being a member of God's people that he could hope to know God and share his life. This was the meaning of the rite of circumcision: it was the ceremony by which the descendant of Abraham was actually incorporated into God's people, the way of access to, and the visible sign of, fellowship with God in and through membership of God's chosen people.

In the Service of Mankind

For the Israelite, this corporate life of communion with God was bounded by the limits of his own people. It rested exclusively on descent from Abraham and on incorporation into the Israelite nation through the rite of circumcision. This we can easily understand, since God's immediate purpose in his dealings with the Israelites was to establish them firmly as a single, distinct people. If this aim was to be achieved, a highly developed national consciousness had to be formed among them. Nevertheless, in calling and forming this people, God had a wider purpose in view. Through Israel God wished to save all mankind. Israel certainly received very special privileges, but, like all God's favours to men, these privileges were not intended exclusively for the benefit of those who received them. Israel's special calling, so far from isolating it from the rest of men, put it rather at the service of the entire human race, and the favours it received were the endowments enabling it to fulfil its appointed task. The fellowship with God into which it had been called was in God's design to be the nucleus of a universal fellowship in which Israel, while retaining the honour of being God's chosen instrument, would share all its privileges with the nations of the earth and, in so doing, achieve its own fulfilment.

The servant of Yahweh, Isaiah tells us, has been appointed by God to be not only 'a covenant to the people', that is, a bond of union between God and Israel, but also 'a light to the nations'. It is his destiny 'to open the eyes that are blind, to bring out the prisoners from the dungeons, from the prison those who sit in darkness',[9] expressions that in biblical language refer to the non-Israelite nations. In a text of Isaiah quoted earlier we saw that Israel was conscious of such a world-wide mission: Mount Sion would one day be a source of the love of God for all mankind. In the meantime, however, Israel was already a sign to the world of the future world-wide people of God. It was a witness to the nations of the unifying, sanctifying and saving power of the one true God. What God had done and was doing for Israel, he would one day do for mankind as a whole.

The Messiah, Head of God's People

We have dwelt at some length on Israel's vocation, and particularly on its corporate life. This seemed necessary for a true understanding of the Church, which is so deeply rooted in Old Testament history. One thing in particular has now emerged clearly. When the Messiah finally came, he came

---

[9] *Is.* 42:6, 7.

as the fulfilment of a people's destiny. He summed up and
embodied in himself all that Israel had hoped for, all that
it had, however imperfectly, already possessed. In the light
of what had gone before, it is inconceivable that he should
have presented himself in any other role but as head of
God's people. Nothing could be more absurd than to try,
as did Harnack and the Liberal Protestants, for example,
around the turn of the century, to interpret him as a preacher
of individual holiness, of private religion resting simply on
filial love of the Father. Set against the history of the people
of Israel, which had for so many centuries been conscious
of being God's people, such an idea simply does not make
sense. He who represented the climax of Israel's hopes could
not possibly come to proclaim the dissolution of its corporate
bonds. On Mount Sinai God had gathered the Israelites
together by his word, and with that gathering their existence
as a people had begun. Henceforward they were intensely
conscious of being God's *ekklēsia*, that is, the assembly called
together by, and deriving its life from, the word of God.
Israel, in other words, was already a Church – the English
equivalent of the Greek *ekklēsia* – in Old Testament times,
and could not think of itself as being anything other than a
Church. When, therefore, the Messiah, the supreme object
of its hope, appeared, he came inevitably as one standing at
the head of a Church, the Church of God's holy people.
When Christ, therefore, gathered disciples around him and
spoke of building a Church, he was acting in accordance
with the genuine messianic hope of Israel.

A New People

It is clear that this Church which Christ founded was
established by him on already existing foundations. For all
its originality, it was, and had to be, in continuity with what
had preceded it. In a sense it was one Church with that of the
Old Testament, inasmuch as it was part of the same plan of
God to gather all mankind into one. In it the Church of the
Old Testament achieved fulfilment. In another sense,

however, it was something completely and astonishingly new. Its newness consisted, first of all, in its being based on a new covenant, a new pact between God and man established through the reconciling act of Christ's passion and death. By the covenant of Sinai God had fashioned a people for himself, but now this covenant has been superseded and God has acquired a new people through the redemptive sacrifice of Christ on Calvary, a people bought with the precious blood of his own Son. In another sense, too, the Church established by Christ was new: unlike the Church of the Old Testament it opened its doors without distinction of race to all mankind. 'This is my blood of the covenant, which is poured out for *many*,' said Christ at the Last Supper, the word 'many', in accordance with common biblical usage, being the equivalent of 'all'. There is now 'neither Jew nor Greek, there is neither slave nor free, there is neither male nor female', for henceforward all are 'one in Christ Jesus' and God has 'visited the Gentiles, to take out of them a people for his name.'[10] The Church of Christ is new, too, in that in Christ and his work mankind has reached new, undreamt-of heights. In Christ, the true eternal Son of God has come on earth, and has made it possible for men to share in his Sonship, to enter into that intimacy with the Father which is his from eternity and to which he alone can give access.

Foundation of the Church: Four Stages

To understand what kind of reality is the Church established by Christ, it is necessary to consider briefly the various acts or stages by which it came into being. Four such stages may be distinguished: the calling, training and sending of the apostles; the paschal mystery, i.e. the passion, death and glorification of Jesus; the institution of the blessed Eucharist; the sending of the holy Spirit on the disciples. In the tract *De Ecclesia* such as we have known it in recent times, only the first of these headings receives any serious

---

[10]*Mark* 14:24; *Gal.* 3:28; *Acts* 15:14.

consideration. This, of course, is to be attributed to the specifically apologetic purpose of the tract, which was never intended to provide an adequate treatment of the Church, though this fact was all too often lost sight of.

In calling and training his apostles, Christ intended that they should form a nucleus around which, after he had returned to the Father, his Church or messianic community would gather. They constituted a distinct group having their own special name, 'the Twelve', and receiving a great deal of special instruction. They enjoyed the closest intimacy with Jesus: as his 'friends' he revealed to them all that he had heard from the Father,[11] including much that had remained hidden from the multitude of his disciples and from the Jewish people in general. During his own lifetime Jesus already gave them a share in his distinctive messianic functions: preaching the coming of God's kingdom, casting out devils, healing the sick, raising the dead to life. This, however, was only the prelude to a definitive commission which they were to discharge after his ascension. For before he departed from them the risen Jesus told them that they were to be witnesses to him 'in Jerusalem and in all Judea and Samaria and to the end of the earth.'[12] By this witness they would create the messianic community, the assembly of those who believed that God had raised up Jesus from the dead and willed to give all men a share in his glorious life, the life of perfect fellowship with himself. Elsewhere, the implications of this mission of the apostles are indicated more fully. 'All authority in heaven and on earth has been given to me', Jesus said to them. 'Go therefore and make disciples of all nations, baptizing them in the name of the Father and of the Son and of the holy Spirit, teaching them to observe all that I have commanded you; and lo, I am with you always, even to the close of the age.'[13] Giving the apostles a share in his own messianic authority, and

---

[11] *John* 15:15.
[12] *Acts* 1:8.
[13] *Matt.* 28:18-20.

ultimately in the authority of the Father himself, Christ here commissions them to gather disciples around them, to bind to themselves, and so to him who has sent them, men and women from every nation of the earth. Making disciples evidently involves teaching the good news of the kingdom. As is explicitly stated, it also involves baptism, which is the rite of initiation into the messianic community and the source for the believer of the life of the risen Christ. Further, it involves teaching the disciples to observe all Christ's instructions, in other words, the exercise of pastoral care, by which the disciples are to be guided and directed in carrying out the practical demands of the Gospel.

Three basic functions are hereby committed to the apostles: teaching or preaching with authority, baptizing, ruling the Christian community. Through the exercise of these functions, they will assemble the Church and form its members according to the mind of Christ. Around them and, as the reference to the end of the age implies, in due course around their successors, will gather the holy community which draws its life from word and sacrament, the twofold means by which the revelation of God in Christ is effectively communicated to mankind. At the heart of the apostolic group and of the entire community stands the chief apostle, Peter. He is the central, essential point of reference for the faith and order of the Church. To him was committed by Christ the supreme pastoral care of the entire believing community. Only in communion with him in unity of faith and acceptance of his pastoral authority is it possible to belong fully to the Church of Christ.

During his earthly life Jesus devoted himself to the training of his apostles with a view to their mission to the world. Without his passion, death and resurrection, however – his paschal mystery as it is called – the Church would have remained an unfulfilled project. The entire purpose of the life of Jesus was to afford a perfect response of love on behalf of mankind to the advances of divine love made in revelation. Revelation, as we have seen, was given in its fulness to the human consciousness of Jesus. By every conscious act of his life, Jesus gave the fullest possible response to the revealing God. His sole concern in all that he did was to give glory to the Father and to accomplish the Father's will in loving obedience. As the pattern of his life unfolded before him, and the full demands of the Father's will gradually took more explicit shape, Jesus gave the ever deeper response which was called for, sounding new depths in the fellowship which bound him inseparably to the Father. It was only on Calvary, however, that the climax of this development was reached. In his passion and death he experienced the full reality of the Father's loving designs for the salvation of the world, and he committed himself totally to their fulfilment. By the supreme act of love whereby he sacrificed himself to the uttermost for his brethren, he completed his earthly course and passed over to the Father, to complete fellowship with him in glory. In this he acted for mankind as a whole, having been appointed by the Father as the New Adam through whom the corporate fall of the first Adam would be repaired. Passing over through the cross and resurrection to the life of glory which constitutes the fulness of the messianic blessings, he wills to bring with him all those who freely unite themselves to him in faith and love. It is in this new life, characterized by a love that triumphs over sin and death, that the inner reality of fellowship in the Church of Christ consists. A share in it has been made possible for mankind through the paschal mystery, which thereby clearly emerges as an essential moment, indeed the central and decisive act, in the establishing of the Church.

A further element in the foundation of the Church is the institution of the blessed Eucharist. On the eve of his passion, Christ bequeathed the Eucharist to his disciples as an abiding memorial of his sacrifice. Under the appearances of bread and wine he placed on the table of the Last Supper, and gave to the twelve to consume, his body and blood which were now pledged to the sacrifice of reconciliation on the cross. By empowering the apostles to renew continually this sacred meal and the reality it contained, he ensured that this sacrifice would never cease to be present in the Church. In all ages and in all places it would be possible, through the Eucharist, for those who believed in him, to associate themselves sacramentally with the supreme act of love on Calvary by which he reconciled mankind to God. What he himself had achieved in principle on the cross for the entire human race could be ratified and actually appropriated by individuals by gathering to participate in the Eucharist. Later, we shall consider more fully the significance of the Eucharist as the centre of Christian worship. It is sufficient to note here that in the Eucharist the faithful offer with Christ the sacrifice of the cross and thereby share in its benefits. These benefits they receive most abundantly when, by receiving Holy Communion, they are personally united to the risen Christ and are taken up by him into his new life of glory and triumphant love. It is in this act that they enter most fully into the fellowship of the Church.

We have considered the role of the apostles, the paschal mystery and the Eucharist in the founding of the Church. Before the Church could come into being as a living reality, however, it had to receive the Spirit of Christ. Prior to the coming of the Spirit, the Church was a lifeless structure, incapable of carrying out the mission entrusted to it. Everything was in readiness for this mission: Christ had died for our sins, the apostles had received their sacred powers, baptism and the Eucharist had been instituted; but as long as the Spirit of life had not come these factors could not achieve their proper effects. On Pentecost Sunday the Spirit came in a whirlwind of power and life, and from that moment the Church was launched on its onward path through the world and through history. This Spirit was the Spirit of Christ, and he was come to complete the work of Christ, to spread abroad throughout the length and breadth of the human race the saving effects of Christ's death and resurrection. Already in the Old Testament the Spirit was foreshadowed in the activities there ascribed to the Spirit of God, e.g. the creation of the world, the giving of life, the exercise of moral influence on the human heart. With the incarnation, however, the personal Spirit of God comes into the world as the guiding principle of the earthly life of Jesus, and when Jesus returns to the Father as the head of a humanity reconciled to God, the Spirit which was hitherto his exclusive possession becomes the common possession of his brethren. This happens at Pentecost, when he sends the Spirit to his assembled disciples. The effects of the Spirit's coming are manifested immediately in the transformation which overtakes the apostles. Filled with new courage and resolution, they go forth to preach the Gospel, setting the Church on the first steps of the path which was to take it to the ends of the earth to gather all nations into its fellowship. In and through the Spirit Christ is present with them as he had promised. Through their preaching, pastoral care and sacramental ministry, all of which are exercised in the power of the Spirit, he brings to fruition in the elect the messianic blessings he had won for mankind on Calvary.

The consciousness of possessing this Spirit of Christ and of God was the dominating experience of the early Christian community. Both in the public life of the Church and in the private life of individual Christians the Spirit was understood to be the supreme moving and guiding force, and the effects of his presence were everywhere clearly perceived. It was this experience of the Spirit that assured the primitive community that God had in truth raised up Jesus and established him as Lord of creation and history, that Jesus was indeed the long-awaited Messiah and that through him the promised messianic blessings were being bestowed. For a regular theme of Old Testament prophecy was that in the messianic times God would pour out his Spirit on mankind in abundance, thereby giving them a new and unbreakable intimacy with himself. Not until the Second Coming of Christ would this intimacy be fully and definitively realized, but in the meantime the Church, through the gift

of the Spirit, already afforded it in no small measure to
believers.

Visible People and Invisible Fellowship

What came into existence as a result of the acts of Jesus
briefly examined above was a visible community or people,
the people of God of the New Testament. This community,
as will be evident from what has been said, is united by
visible bonds: the word of God preached by the apostles
and accepted and publicly professed in faith; participation
in the eucharistic celebration, for which baptism is the
initiation and which is the distinctive community act of
worship of the new *ekklēsia*; fellowship with the apostles, the
recognized leaders of the community. We find all this clearly
expressed in the second chapter of the Acts of the Apostles:
'Now when they (i.e. the Jews) heard this they were cut to
the heart and said to Peter and the rest of the apostles,
"Brethren what shall we do?", and Peter said to them,
"Repent, and be baptized every one of you, in the name of
Jesus Christ for the forgiveness of your sins; and you shall
receive the gift of the holy Spirit" . . . So those who received
his word were baptized, and there were added that day
about three thousand souls. And they devoted themselves
to the apostles' teaching and fellowship, to the breaking of
bread and the prayers.'[14]

All this outward framework, however – it can be summed
up in the threefold heading of Word, Sacrament and
authoritative Office – is the expression of an inner reality,
in itself the heart of the Church's life: the risen life of
Christ communicated to the Church by the Spirit of Christ
as the common possession of all the baptized. 'We were
buried therefore with him (i.e. Christ) by baptism into
death,' says St Paul, 'so that as Christ was raised from the
dead by the glory of the Father, we too, might walk in
newness of life.'[15] This new life, common life in the Body of

[14]*Acts* 2:37f.
[15]*Rom.* 6:4.

G

Christ, is the substance of the messianic blessings so eagerly awaited, the true fulfilment of the life of the people of God of the Old Testament. In it is fulfilled the celebrated prophecy of Jeremiah: 'This is the covenant I will make with the house of Israel after those days, says the Lord; I will put my law within them, and I will write it upon their hearts, and I will be their God, and they shall be my people.'[16] The outward fellowship of the Church is of value only in so far as it expresses and promotes this inner communion with Christ. Since it does in fact, however, fulfil these functions, it is an indispensable, integral, inseparable part of the Church Christ founded.

Common Life in the Spirit

Guided by the teaching of the Second Vatican Council, the Church is today acquiring a more adequate self-understanding. In particular a new awareness is emerging of what it means for the Church to be the people of God. One of the most valuable insights this concept has to offer is an appreciation of Christian existence as existence in the Spirit of Christ. As a people the Church possesses its own characteristic way of life, and this is defined with reference to the Spirit who vivifies it. The way of life of God's people is life in the Spirit. This is the antithesis of the selfish, sinful life which is ours by nature, what St Paul terms life 'according to the flesh'. It is the work of the Spirit to overcome this fleshly life by implanting in men's hearts the love of Christ. The Spirit creates the new, spiritual man, whose life is the outgoing, self-sacrificing life of redemptive love, communicated to him by the risen Christ. As Christ delivered himself to death 'for the redemption of many', so the Christian is by definition one who accepts responsibility for the salvation of others and does not refuse to carry their burdens. The Christian life consists of an unending series of 'spiritual sacrifices', that is, sacrifices which, precisely because of the Spirit who energizes and inspires them, are

---

[16] *Jer.* 31:33.

true and genuine, find acceptance with God and win his mercy for sinners. Prayer, almsgiving, thanksgiving, penance, witness, good works of all kinds – these are the sacrifices which the Christian offers as the normal fruit of life in the Church.

It is much to be desired that we recover the vivid experience of possessing the Spirit enjoyed by the early Christians, that we become more deeply aware of life in Christ as life in Christ's Spirit. In this way, our Christian existence will become the vital and dynamic reality it ought to be, the source of joy, peace, gentleness, kindness, confidence and all the other 'fruits of the Spirit' which should characterize the Christian. For a full understanding of this Spirit-directed life, it would be necessary to study in detail the letters of St Paul. Subsequent chapters in this book will have much light to throw on it. In the meantime, the following passage from St Paul's epistle to the Colossians will help to convey its general character:

Put on then, as God's chosen ones, holy and beloved, compassion, kindness, lowliness, meekness and patience, forbearing one another and, if one has a complaint against another, forgiving each other; as the Lord has forgiven you, so you also must forgive. And above all these put on love, which binds everything together in perfect harmony. And let the peace of Christ rule in your hearts, to which indeed you were called in the one Body. And be thankful. Let the word of Christ dwell in you richly, as you teach and admonish one another in all wisdom, and as you sing psalms and hymns and spiritual songs with thankfulness in your hearts to God. And whatever you do, in word or deed, do everything in the name of the Lord Jesus, giving thanks to God the Father through him.[17]

It is not only to the individual, however, that the Spirit of Christ is given. The Church as a whole too, must become more conscious of being led by the Spirit as it proceeds on

[17]*Col.* 3:12-17.

its pilgrim way through history. In the midst of weakness
and suffering the Spirit assures it of final victory, leading it
on to the definitive union with Christ in the glorious fellowship of the final kingdom.

The Body of Christ

Because the life of the people of God is life in the Spirit
of Christ, this people may also be described as the Body of
Christ. By this is meant that Christ's followers are in a
mysterious sense an extension of Christ himself, that they
share his life, his privileges and his destiny. In this sense
they are, in the words of St Paul, 'one person'[18] with him,
or, in Hebrew idiom, 'one body', body in Hebrew denoting
the individual person considered as visibly and tangibly
present. It is important to note that this phrase 'Body of
Christ' has, as used by St Paul, a strong eucharistic reference:
'The bread which we break,' he writes to the Corinthians,
'is it not a participation in the Body of Christ? Because there
is one loaf, we who are many are one Body, for we all
partake of the same loaf.'[19] St Paul here passes imperceptibly
from the idea of the eucharistic to that of the mystical Body
of Christ. He can do so because it is by receiving Christ in
the Eucharist that we are made one with him; in other words,
it is by eating the (eucharistic) Body of Christ that we
become the (mystical) Body of Christ.

We shall return to this idea in the chapter on the Liturgy.
Meanwhile, we should note its importance for the renewal of
ecclesiology. It points the way to the restoration of a
neglected heritage. In patristic times, Church and Eucharist
were seen in close association. The most striking expression
of this was the use of the term 'Body of Christ'. On the one
hand it was applied to the Church, as St Paul had applied
it originally. On the other hand it was applied to the
Eucharist, but with the addition of the adjective 'mystical':
the Church was the true Body of Christ, the Eucharist his

---

[18]*Gal.* 3:28.
[19]I *Cor.* 10:16f.

mystical Body, the latter phrase designating both the new mode of existence of the risen Christ and his veiled presence in the sacrament. It was quite clear, however, that Church and Eucharist were bound together in a mutually creative interchange. The Eucharist was the communal celebration of the Lord's Supper by the Christian community. As such it was completely dependent on the Church. In the Eucharist, on the other hand, the Church actualized itself in a unique manner. From this source it continually replenished the life of the Spirit which animated it and its members. So obvious was this connection between Church and Eucharist in patristic times, and so firm the grasp of its consequences, that membership of the Church was identified with participation in the eucharistic celebration. Not only was access to the Eucharist restricted to members of the Church, but the Church was regarded as essentially eucharistic fellowship, both at the local and the world-wide level.[20] It was the assembly of those who gathered at regular intervals to partake of the Lord's Body. There the Lord presided over his own, renewing in them faith, hope and charity through the life-giving channels of word and sacrament. Wherever the Eucharist was celebrated, it was the same Lord who was host of the table and the same fellowship that was being established.

Within this fellowship there was, of course, orderly arrangement of ministries. In each Church this took place under the direction of the bishop, who was himself the leader of the assembly as well as the link guaranteeing the unity of the local Eucharist with the Church universal. It was against this background that Order or Office was seen. It had its place emphatically within the context of the brotherhood of the eucharistic assembly. This is not to say that it was confined in its exercise to the Liturgy itself. Rather did the Liturgy, precisely as supreme manifestation of the Church, clearly exhibit the hierarchical arrangement

---

[20]Cf. L. Hertling, S.J., *Communio. Chiesa e papato nell' antichità cristiana*, Rome 1961.

which was essential to the Church and as such was a permanent and continuous feature of its life. However, the
liturgical, eucharistic context pointed the way to a true
understanding of Office. It manifested its subordinate role
in relation to word and sacrament, the creative sources of the
Church's life. And it indicated the spirit of charity, humility
and brotherhood with which it was to be exercised: among
the guests gathered around the table of the Lord the exercise
of authority could not constitute a claim to dominance over
others; it was rather a call to become, both in reality and in
the eyes of men, as 'he that serveth', after the example of
Christ in the Supper Room who knelt to wash the feet of his
disciples.

In the course of time, however, the interdependence of
Church and Eucharist was gradually obscured. Owing to a
pre-occupation with the Real Presence of Christ in the
Eucharist, a doctrine denied by Berengarius of Tours in the
eleventh century, the words 'true' and 'mystical' as applied
to Church and Eucharist were interchanged. The Eucharist
came to be known as the true Body of Christ, the Church
as the mystical Body. In this new context the adjective
'mystical' was loosed from its original sacramental moorings
and came to be understood as a synonym of figurative, or
unreal. The Church came more and more to be understood
as Body of Christ in a metaphorical sense, in the sense, to
be precise, of a moral body or corporation. This brought
with it a pronounced shift of emphasis: the sacramental
viewpoint was overshadowed by the juridical, while secular
concepts of power came to exercise a regrettable influence
on the understanding of Church authority.[21] Today the
Church still suffers from the effects of this distortion. Nevertheless, it is rapidly regaining a more profound understanding
of the nature of the authority committed to it by Christ.

The return to the patristic understanding of the Church

---

[21]Cf. J. Ratzinger, 'The Pastoral Implications of Episcopal Collegiality',
Concilium, January 1965, 20-32; *id.*, 'Zeichen unter den Volkern', in M.
Schmaus – A. Läpple (ed.), *Wahrheit und Zeugnis*, Düsseldorf 1964, 456-66.

as eucharistic communion, which is now under way, will
prove to be one of the most powerful factors in this development. By linking all authority in the Church to the task of
witnessing faithfully to the word of God and of ensuring the
fitting celebration of the liturgy, it will help to commend
to a generation that tends to view authority in any form
with a jaundiced eye the exercise of spiritual rule by the
apostolic college. On the other hand it will provide in the
idea of eucharistic brotherhood a powerful inspiration for
the exercise of authority in a truly Christian style.

A further aspect of St Paul's doctrine of the Body of
Christ calls for mention. With the idea of eucharistic Body
St Paul closely associates that of the human body considered
as a unified organism composed of many different members.[22]
To describe the Church as Christ's Body has therefore a
further meaning: each individual Christian has his own
special role to play in the Christian community, and the
good of the entire community depends in some measure
on his fidelity to this calling. It is by the harmonious fulfilment of the difficult demands of diversity and unity,
apparently conflicting but in reality mutually complementary, that the welfare and vigour of the Church is secured.
Once again it is the Spirit of Christ who ensures this
harmony. He is on the one hand the Spirit of unity and
order, on the other hand the Spirit of diversity and freedom.
From this point of view too, it is necessary that the role of
the Spirit in the Church be more fully understood and
appreciated than it has been in the recent past.

We have seen above that the sending of the holy Spirit
was a constitutive factor in the founding of the Church.
This means that while the Spirit exercises his role in the
Church in harmony and co-operation with the mission of
the hierarchy – also, as we have seen, a constitutive element
of the Church – he is not tied in his activity to hierarchical
channels. The Church knows not only Office but charisms,

---

[22] 1 Cor. 12:27.

the free, unpredictable gifts of the holy Spirit. The welfare of the Church is dependent on both alike. It pertains to Office to provide for the free growth and orderly functioning of charisms. All that can contribute to the building up of the Church must be welcomed, in whatever part of the Christian community it appears. The holy Spirit is at work throughout the entire people of God and his guidance of the Church is exercised not only through the rule of the hierarchy but also through the experience and insight of the faithful. Hence, the grave need for as full as possible an exchange of views within the Church and for suitable structures through which it can take place.

All that we have seen in this chapter may be summed up as follows: the Church is the people of God which exists under the form of the Body of Christ through the power of the holy Spirit. In the following chapter a discussion of two community virtues, justice and charity, will throw further light on the meaning of the common life of this holy people.

Charity and Justice:
Common Life in Christ

Denis O'Callaghan

The God/man relationship which is the Christian life is situated in a community. God approaches man in community; man finds God in community. In this the particular character of the Christian life follows the ordinary pattern of human life. Man is a person but a person in community. He is born into the varied context of human relationship; he creates himself as a fully mature and developed person in and through these relationships. This being in community is not merely a matter of being surrounded by others, of other people happening to be where he is. It is the simple fact that life in community makes man everything that we know him to be. He owes to the community his attitudes and institutions, his ideas and language, his values and ideals. In the classical definition of the person one is inclined to emphasize what is original, individual, and incommunicable in him. One may forget that what is derived, what is common, and what is shared is of equal importance in his make-up.

Man's life in Christ follows a similar pattern. He is baptized into the community of God's people, he receives the faith of the believing community, he prays with the worshipping community, he returns for forgiveness of sin to the redeemed community. The only morality and religion that we know occur in this community context and are to be analysed in relation to it. An ethical or mystical emphasis is false if it is so concerned with the idea of the individual isolated in solitary relationship with God that men are seen as outsiders and intruders. Christ's own life was that of a man among men, concerned with their needs corporal and spiritual. In setting out to alter the destiny of the community of mankind he made common cause with man and was himself caught up in their destiny.

If to a great extent Christian life is community life, then to the same extent Christian virtue is community virtue. The terms between which the full range of community virtue may be plotted are charity and justice. These set the tension of community morality. Charity is the ideal or theme of the Christian life. It is an open, flexible, generous virtue. It moves action wherever it observes need; it does not count the cost; it does not expect a return. Justice is a closed, rigid, minimal virtue. It takes account only of the actual rights of another; it draws a clear line between thine and mine; it requires that everyone get his strict due, neither more nor less.

In comparison between the 'open' virtue of charity and the 'limit' virtue of justice the latter generally suffers. The former paints the broad sweep of an inspired community morality, while the latter appears more earthbound and tends to haggle about details. But both are essential for responsible community action. Moral responsibility must take account of *all* the values of the situation. It must take account of the fact that man is an incarnate being surrounded by other similar beings in a material world. All this qualifies the pattern of charity among men. Unless charity is underpinned by limit virtues, such as truth, justice, chastity, it becomes a vague, vagrant, formless attitude. If it does not take human nature and the given context of human action seriously, it is not realistic and does not deserve the name of virtue.

The highlight of Christ's moral teaching in the New

Testament is the promulgation of the commandment of
love. But when the Pharisees heard that he had silenced
the Sadducees, they came together. And one of them, a
lawyer, asked him a question, to test him. 'Teacher, which
is the great commandment of the law?' And he said to
him, 'You shall love the Lord your God with all your
heart, with all your soul, and with all your mind. This is
the great and first commandment. And a second is like it,
you shall love your neighbour as yourself. On these two
commandments depend all the law and the prophets.'[1]

The precept of love with this double term is a single
commandment, the *new* commandment, the message of
Christ for Christian living. It is spelled out in the radical
demands of the Sermon on the Mount, it is recalled to the
apostles' memory in the Last Supper Discourse, it is underlined in the teaching of the apostles, above all in the epistles
of St John. This commandment was personified in Christ.
He loved his Father in the identity of a single principle of
life. 'I and the Father are one.'[2] He loved his human brethren
to the point of becoming one with them. 'As as you did it to
one of the least of these my brethren, you did it to me.'[3]

Christ gave to Christians this same mission of love. It is
not simply a matter of changing old attitudes, it is a matter of
changing old natures. It is not a 'thou shalt', it is a 'thou
art'. The message is contained in his action of drawing the
human race into the love-life of the Trinity and making of
them there a single family. In virtue of this action one
addresses God as Father and Christ as brother, and in
Christ one calls all men brethren. There is no point in using
these terms unless one acts in accordance with them by
having for God a love similar to that of a child for parent, and
for one's fellowman a love similar to that of brother for
brother.

---

[1] *Matt.* 22:34-40.
[2] *John* 10:30.
[3] *Matt.* 25:40.

Both elements of Christ's commandment of love already occur in the Old Testament. In fact, St Luke puts this commandment in the mouth of the lawyer in answer to Christ's question: 'What is written in the law?'[4] The direction, You shall love the Lord your God with all your heart, and with all your soul, and with all your mind, is the first sentence of the *Shema Israel* (Hear, O Israel), the confession of faith recited morning and evening by the devout Jew.[5] The direction, You shall love your neighbour as yourself, is part of the Torah given by God to Moses in Leviticus.[6] The search for a commandment which would sum up the whole law and the prophets was familiar to pre-Christian Judaism. There were many suggestions as to what the unifying principle might be. The great Rabbi Hillel (c. 20 B.C.) recognized it in a negative version of the Golden Rule; the positive version is familiar to us from Christ's words: 'So whatever you wish that men would do to you, do so to them; for this is the law and the prophets.'[7]

The fact that these traces of the commandment of love can be found outside Christian sources does not take from the originality of Christ's message. Even though the material terms occur elsewhere the significance which Christ attaches to them is uniquely his own.

In Christ's mind the love which man shows to God and neighbour is not only a moral act, it is a religious act; it is his response to God's love for him, because God loved first. In this response to God the two commandments of love are linked; the love of God finds expression and proves itself in brotherly love. This linking is expressed in Christ's direction that before offering sacrifice to God one should make peace with one's neighbours,[8] and in the admonition attached to the Lord's Prayer: 'If you forgive men their trespasses, your

---

[4] *Luke* 10:26.
[5] *Deut.* 6:4-5.
[6] *Lev.* 19:18.
[7] *Matt.* 7:12.
[8] *Matt.* 5:24.

heavenly Father also will forgive you.'[9] St John understood
well that this was what Christ intended: 'Beloved, if God so
loved us, we also ought to love one another. No man has
ever seen God; if we love one another, God abides in us and
his love is perfected in us . . . We love, because he first loved
us. If anyone says "I love God", and hates his brother, he is a
liar; for he who does not love his brother whom he has seen,
cannot love God whom he has not seen.'[10] This linking
receives particular point in Christ, the meeting-point of
God and man. The invitation of love goes out from God to
men through Christ, and back to God through Christ. 'As
the Father has loved me, so have I loved you'; 'If a man
loves me, he will keep my word, and my Father will love
him'; 'Whoever receives one such child in my name receives
me, and whoever receives me, receives not me, but him who
sent me.'[11]

Christ universalized the idea of neighbour. In the commandment of love in Leviticus, neighbour is defined as a
fellow-Israelite, 'the son of your own people'.[12] It is true
that later on in this same chapter of Leviticus we read: 'The
stranger who sojourns with you shall be to you as the native
among you, and you shall love him as yourself; for you were
strangers in the land of Egypt.'[13] The generous character of
this statement was qualified in Jewish attitude and practice,
for example, *stranger* was taken to refer to the proselyte, or,
where it is clear that a pagan is concerned, charity was to
be extended to him for the sake of peace and good order in
the community. At any rate, the *strangers* who were to be
treated with kindness and equity were not men in general
but only those who were domiciled or who sojourned among
the Israelites. The law of usury indicates marked bias even
against those non-Israelites: 'To a foreigner you may lend

[9]*Matt.* 6:14.
[10]1 *John* 4:11-20.
[11]*John* 15:9; 14:23; *Mark* 9:37.
[12]*Lev.* 19:18.
[13]*Lev.* 19:34.

upon interest, but to your brother you shall not lend upon interest.'[14]

For the Israelites God was primarily the God of the Covenant and they were the race chosen from among the unbelieving nations. They were slow in accepting the consequences of the doctrine that all men were made in God's image and that this should inspire a universal love. According to Jewish sources the Rabbi Ben Azzai (A.D. 100) seems to have been the first to formulate this conviction.[15] The Stoic ideal of universal humanism was influential in bringing Hellenistic Judaism to accept this belief.

For Christ there is no limitation. Christian love extends to all men; it is co-terminous with the love of God who created all men and who makes his sun to rise upon all equally, the good and the bad; it is co-terminous with the love of Christ who died for all men and calls all men brothers. It is stronger than human love because it embraces not only friends and those to whom one is drawn by natural affinity, but also enemies and those from whom one is repelled by natural antipathy. Christ does not delay over the psychological problems that loving one's enemies may involve. It seems obvious that he would not give much of a hearing to the suggestion that *loving* them does not mean *liking* them. The love of which he speaks is so deeply inspired that it neutralizes and surges over the petty boundaries which natural feelings tend to draw. The Christian who loves as Christ loved experiences how irrelevant these boundaries are. No one is to be excluded from Christian love, no matter of what colour, race, or creed, and no matter how ungrateful he proves. Christian love is completely generous, it is prodigal by conventional standards, it hopes for nothing in return.

Love your enemies, do good to those who hate you, bless those who curse you, pray for those who abuse you . . . If

---

[14]*Deut.* 23:20.
[15]See Rudolf Schnackenburg, *The Moral Teaching of the New Testament*, London 1964, 97.

you love those who love you, what credit is that to you? For even sinners love those who love them. And if you do good to those who do good to you, what credit is that to you? For even sinners do the same. And if you lend to those from whom you hope to receive, what credit is that to you? Even sinners lend to sinners, to receive as much again. But love your enemies, and do good, and lend, expecting nothing in return; and your reward will be great, and you will be sons of the Most High; for he is kind to the ungrateful and selfish. Be merciful, even as your Father is merciful.[16]

The radical character of the demands of the Sermon on the Mount (turning the other cheek, handing over one's cloak to one who takes one's coat, going two miles with the traveller who forces you to go one) all show that a new ideal has come into human life, something which is incomprehensible to man closed up in his selfish worldliness. This ideal contradicts the ordinary tendencies of human nature, and so the Christian is ever tempted to slip back into conventional attitudes. Already in the first generation of Christianity we find worldly attitudes creeping into the community of charity. St James has this complaint:

My brethren, show no partiality as you hold the faith of Our Lord Jesus Christ, the Lord of glory. For if a man with gold rings and in fine clothing comes into your assembly, and a poor man in shabby clothing also comes in, and you pay attention to the one who wears the fine clothing and say, 'Have a seat here, please,' while you say to the poor man, 'Stand there,' or 'Sit at my feet,' have you not made distinctions among yourselves?[17]

In giving this commandment of love, Christ makes his own love the love which we must imitate. 'Love one another, as I have loved you.'[18] This is just as unattainable as that

[16]*Luke* 6:27-36.
[17]*Jas.* 2:1-4.
[18]*John* 13:34.

other direction 'You must be perfect, as your heavenly
Father is perfect,'[19] but it is the ideal at which the Christian
must aim. The Christian is called on to love to the extent of
God's own love, excluding no one. He is called on to love
with the intensity of God's love, losing himself in devotedness
to God and to his fellowmen. Since he can never meet this
ideal, he will never be satisfied with the extent or quality
of his love. For this reason, humility is built into Christian
love. It is always the love of the Publican, never that of
the Pharisee.

The New Testament background provides us with an
insight into the place and meaning of charity in the Christian
life. Charity draws its inspiration from faith. It is an attitude
formed from an appreciation of what God is and what man
is in relation to God. But it is not just an intellectual conviction. It is a living force which alters one's whole life and
inspires one's actions. In this connection we speak of the
primacy of charity. St Paul sets the theme of the Christian
life with the words: 'Above all these put on love.'[20] This
over-all quality of charity does not mean that it dispenses
with moral rules or laws. Christ stated that he did not come
to set aside the law and the prophets. God's commandments
would still have full force in his kingdom.[21] In the Sermon
on the Mount he accepts the decalogue as his starting point,
but he goes on to show that the material observance of these
rules is not sufficient, the interior disposition of heart is the
decisive factor; in lusting for another's wife a man has
already committed adultery with her in his heart.[22]

Charity, then, makes the laws of the decalogue its own.
They become the laws of love. When St Paul refers to
charity as the fulness of the law it is significant that he
implies this to emphasize the obligations of justice.[23] In an

---

[19]*Matt.* 5:48.
[20]*Col.* 3:14.
[21]*Matt.* 5:17-19.
[22]*Matt.* 5:28.
[23]*Rom.* 13:7-10.

ethic of charity the various virtues still preserve their identity. Each of them translates charity into a particular field of human activity – justice provides the substratum of charity in the field of property, chastity provides it in the field of sexuality, truth provides it in the field of communication. Charity would be unrealistic if it ignored the more limited values which provide the guidelines of what is loving action for a human being.

Where lesser virtues are concerned charity intervenes to give them their specifically Christian quality and an over-all direction to the last end. When a number of particular values cross in a situation it is charity which balances them one against the other and decides what Christian action should be. But charity is much more than a control of the other virtues, much more than a direction finder in cases were a number of norms are relevant. The invitation of love comes not just through law but through the individual situation itself. Charity may suggest a line of action which is not obligatory by any general law, but is required of this particular individual in this particular situation. Here we speak of counsel or vocation. If one declines such an invitation, one has failed to rise above one's selfish interest in surrendering oneself to the full response of love. The choice placed before the Rich Young Man in the Gospels is an example of this kind of counsel or vocation.[24] Does a refusal imply sin or guilt? True, the refusal may eventually lead one to exclude God from one's life, but in the ordinary case one is unhappy about using the crude terms, sin and guilt, to characterize this failure of love.

We have said that charity sets the theme of the Christian life in that it introduces that ideal moral quality into it which makes it at once fully human and really Christian. A comparison between justice and charity and an analysis of how charity affects justice will indicate something of the nature of that new quality.

---

[24]*Matt.* 19:16-30; *Mark* 10:17-27; *Luke* 18:18-30.

H

In pre-Christian philosophy justice was accepted as the queen of the virtues. There was good reason for so characterizing it. In guaranteeing that everyone receives that which is due it promotes and protects essential values in private and community life. It safeguards the individual from arbitrary interference by affording him the freedom, security, and means to live his life independently. It protects the community from disorder in that it avoids clashes which would inevitably ensue if each person consulted his own interests and wishes on the principle that might is right. As society becomes more civilized it codifies more carefully and completely the rules of private and community justice. Justice and law are mother and daughter. Law seeks to reflect the canons of that ideal justice which precedes any positive legal system, and in turn the rule of law makes justice concrete in man's everyday dealings.

Justice, then, is an important element in man's moral life, but it is dangerous to regard it as pre-eminent. Even though it is a shield which wards off the grasping hand of the avaricious man, it may also be used as a sword in the merciless demand of one's own rights. *Summum jus, summa injuria;* one can be too just. The demand of the strictly just man is 'pay what you owe'; his justification is 'I am within my rights'. In all justice the priest and the Levite passed the wounded man in the parable of the Good Samaritan; they had not done the injury and so they owed him nothing. On the other hand, a similar extreme view of justice may lead to pointless revenge or to the vicious futility of the vendetta, eye for eye and tooth for tooth.

If justice is to be really human and Christian it must be balanced by the benign influence of charity. Charity makes its influence felt in a number of ways.

Charity saves justice from itself. 'Charity is patient, is kind, is not ambitious, seeketh not her own, is not provoked to anger, thinketh no evil.'[25] It corrects the exaggerations

---

[25] *1 Cor.* 13:4-5 (Douay version).

of blind, instinctive justice. It pricks the conscience of one who is arrogantly just and reminds him that excess in justice is a vice.

Virtus in medio stat is the classical phrase which indicates the range of the moral virtues. The mean or median line of justice is determined by the extent of one's rights, but this does not mean automatically that one has the power to demand one's rights in the concrete situation. Charity recalls one to a recognition of the fact that no virtue exists in a vacuum, that the writ of justice may not be enforced in the face of more primary considerations. Without this controlling influence of charity justice could easily become a cannibal virtue and serve avarice rather than equity. This is the lesson in the gospel story of the merciless servant who failed to show to his own poor debtor some of the indulgence which he had experienced at the hands of his master who had forgiven him a far greater debt.[26]

On many occasions Christ campaigned against the chicanery and hair-splitting which mere mastery of the law provided. The obligation of the sabbath observance was so exaggerated that more basic duties of charity were ignored – Christ stated: 'The sabbath was made for man, not man for the sabbath.'[27] The emphasis on ritual cleanliness was so marked that this was regarded as the means of justification – Christ stated: 'There is nothing outside a man which by going into him can defile him; but the things which come out of a man are what defile him.'[28] A plea that one had vowed one's property as a temple offering (Corban) was suggested as a way of avoiding the duty of supporting one's parents – Christ stated: 'You have a fine way of rejecting the commandment of God, in order to keep your tradition.'[29] The long list of petty legal distinctions in Matthew 23 by which the Scribes and Pharisees distorted and obscured the

---

[26] *Matt.* 18:27-35.
[27] *Mark.* 2:27.
[28] *Mark* 7:15.
[29] *Mark* 7:9.

law of God's love gives body to Christ's charge: 'You
blind guides, straining out a gnat and swallowing a
camel'.

Charity gives new meaning to justice. In natural justice
one respects the rights of the other because he is a human
being and a person; in Christian justice one also respects the
rights of the other as one who is called to a new life in
Christ. The Christian in asking for recognition of his rights
in justice can claim a new title, that of brother, brother not
only in the sense of member of the human race but in the
sense of co-heir of God's kingdom.

Charity is more radical and more far-reaching in the
scale of virtue than justice. It takes account not only of
man's rights but also of his needs. In a way, justice is a
passive virtue. It allows one to sit idly by once strict duty
has been performed. Charity is not so easily satisfied; it is
much more conscious of sins of omission; it cannot sit and
contemplate need; it intervenes readily whenever and
wherever help is required. This force of charity is clearly
illustrated in the parable of the Good Samaritan. "Which
of these three (priest, Levite, Samaritan) do you think,
proved neighbour to the man who fell among robbers?"
He said, "The one who showed mercy on him." And Jesus
said to him, "Go and do likewise."[30] The Last Judgement
discourses show that only those who follow the example of
the Good Samaritan will possess the kingdom of Heaven.[31]
Jesus's closest followers, the apostles, well understood this
lesson. 'By this we know love, that he laid down his life for
us; and we ought to lay down our lives for the brethren. But if
anyone has the world's goods and sees his brother in need,
yet closes his heart against him, how can God's love abide
in him? Little children let us not love in word or speech
but in deed and in truth.'[32] 'If a brother or sister is ill-clad
and in lack of daily food, and one of you says to

[30]*Luke* 10:36-37.
[31]*Matt.* 25.
[32]1 *John* 3:16-18.

them, "Go in peace, be warmed and filled," without giving them the things needed for the body, what does it profit?"[33]

Early Christian teaching on the use of earthly wealth and good fortune was far more conscious of the needs of poverty than of the rights of property. The Fathers did admit that goods belonged radically to the owner, but they saw ownership as a sacred trust by which under the providence of God the goods of the earth are to be used for the benefit of all men. They stated that while a man could own capital or productive property, he was obliged to give to those in need the consumer goods which he did not personally require. Clement of Alexandria directs: 'In place of renouncing possession of one's capital one should renounce the spiritual passions which hinder one from making responsible use of one's property. One should try to purge oneself of selfishness so that one may put the goods in one's possession to the best possible use.'[34] On this principle St Ambrose taught: 'The bread which you hold back is the food of the hungry; the clothes which you store away are the covering of the naked; the money which you bury is a poor man's ransom.'[35]

Where property is concerned one must take account of two kinds of rights. There is a natural right to private property, since this is required to protect the independence of the individual and to enable him to meet his responsibilities and to develop his capabilities as a person. But there is also the natural right of every human being to have access to material goods in order to live in a fashion befitting a human person. If the pattern of ownership makes the realization of this right impossible then this right takes precedence over the right of private property.

---

[33] Jas. 2:15-16.
[34] Quis dives salvetur? PG 9:620.
[35] Ep. 81, quoted in Decretum Gratiani C.8, D.47. On the teaching of the Fathers see Paul Christophe, Les devoirs moraux des riches (l'usage du droit de propriété dans l'Ecriture et la tradition patristique), Paris 1964.

Christian tradition takes a different line according as it
emphasizes one or other of these positions. The text-book
tradition is strong on the rights of the property owner.
Indeed, the treatise *De Iustitia* has been described as an
Owner's Handbook directing how one may obtain, preserve,
and keep others off one's property. On the other side,
the social teaching of the popes has underlined the universal destination of earthly goods and maintained that
the primary purpose of material creation is to serve all
men and all races. Pope Paul's recent encyclical on *The
Development of Peoples*, summing up this tradition, borrows
many of its ideas from Vatican II's *Church in the Modern
World*.

If the world is made to furnish each individual with the
means of livelihood and the instruments for his growth and
progress, each man has therefore the right to find in the
world what is necessary for himself. . . . All other rights
whatsoever, including those of property and free commerce,
are to be subordinated to this principle. They should not
hinder but on the contrary favour its application. It is a
grave and urgent social duty to redirect them to their
primary finality. . . . Private property does not constitute
for anyone an absolute and unconditional right. No one is
justified in keeping for his exclusive use what he does not
need, when others lack necessities. In a word, according to
the traditional doctrine as found in the Fathers of the
Church and the great theologians the right to property
must never be exercised to the detriment of the common
good. If there should arise a conflict between acquired
private rights and primary community exigencies, it is
the responsibility of public authorities to look for the
solution, with the active participation of individuals and
social groups. . . . It is unfortunate that a system has been
constructed which considers profit as the key motive for
economic progress, competition as the supreme law of
economics, and private ownership of the means of pro-

duction as an absolute right that has no limits and carries no corresponding social obligations.[36]

Naturally these positions are not watertight; it is a question of where one places the emphasis. The text-book tradition does not see private property as an absolute right. It admits that the property-owner has social responsibilities, that in face of extreme need material property reverts to its universal or common state. The tradition of the papal encyclicals accepts private property as a natural right, as the way in which the goods of the earth best serve to support mankind, but it emphasizes that the common good of mankind severely limits the extent of this right.

In contemporary discussion on the responsibilities of the person in community, the virtue of social justice comes in for a good deal of consideration. Social justice aims to produce a proper social order, it aims to produce those economic, political, moral, and intellectual conditions and opportunities which will allow all citizens to exercise their fundamental rights and live a human life. So defined it is simply another or more modern term for the general justice of Aristotle and St Thomas, the virtue which tends to promote and preserve the welfare of the community, or the virtue which directs the acts of all other virtues to the common good. Social justice is close kin to equity and to charity. If charity is described as the virtue of community, then social justice is the virtue of society. If society has no other meaning than to serve and give structure to the community, social justice has no other meaning than to translate charity into social action in and through the structures of society.

Social justice is at once the virtue of good government and of good citizenship. It directs public authority to establish those structures and conditions which will allow all citizens to live in freedom and in a properly human fashion. It directs the individual citizen to fulfil his social duties and to take account of the welfare of society in all his actions. The

---

[36]Nos. 22-26, Cf. Constitution *On the Church in the Modern World*, No. 69.

Vatican Council teaches that far too many people are devoid
of social conscience: 'There are those who, while professing,
grand and rather noble sentiments, nevertheless in reality
live always as if they cared nothing for the needs of society.
Many in various places even make light of social laws and
precepts, and do not hesitate to resort to various frauds and
deceptions in avoiding just taxes or other debts due to
society. Others think little of certain norms of social life, for
example, those designed for the protection of health, or
laws establishing speed limits.'[37]

Social conscience is really a sense of community. Where
the production of goods is concerned this means that the
individual capitalist or the employers' association should
not see profit as the only essential element in business; they
must have the welfare of the employees and the general
benefit of the community at heart as well. It will also mean
that the worker or trade unionist does not think only of
better wages and better working conditions without
consideration for the welfare of his industry and of his
country. The appearance of more mature and balanced
attitudes in these respects in recent years is to be welcomed.
A similar social conscience should exist where the use of
property is concerned. The owner who hoards goods for his
exclusive and selfish use, or who squanders property, or who
deliberately destroys food in order to keep prices high is to be
seen in much the same light as the money lender or the
extortioner who grinds the faces of the poor and the unfortunate. All these sin against humanity, against the nature
of property, and against the duty of assisting those in need.
Both the hoarder and the squanderer may say that they are
within their rights in doing what they like with what is their
own. It is true that they do not violate strict justice; they do
not take or injure what actually belongs to another. But
strict justice is only one value, and a limited one at that,
where the use of property is concerned.

---

[37] *On the Church in the Modern World*, No. 30.

In recent years there has developed a widespread awareness that the social question is world-wide, that humanity is one and that the wealthier nations are called on to come to the aid of those in need. Side by side with this there is the awareness that the scandal of men starving and living in inhuman conditions beside their over-fed and opulent neighbours can be solved by combined international effort – if only the squandering of resources and of good-will in misdirected nationalism and in the arms race could be suspended. Christianity would not be true to its Founder, and would not be credible to any thinking man, if it stood apart at this juncture. Again in Pope Paul's words:

Today the people in hunger are making a dramatic appeal to the people blessed with abundance, the Church shudders at this cry of anguish and calls each one to give a loving response to a brother's cry for help. . . . When so many people are hungry, when so many families suffer from destitution, when so many remain steeped in ignorance, when so many schools, hospitals and homes worthy of the name remain to be built, all public or private squandering of wealth, all expenditure prompted by motives of national or personal ostentation, every exhausting armaments race becomes an intolerable scandal. We are conscious of our duty to denounce it. Would that those in authority listened to our words before it is too late.[38]

---

[38] *The Development of Peoples*, No. 53.

Grace:
The Indwelling Trinity

DONAL FLANAGAN

The fundamental Christian mystery, the great and ultimate reality, is the Father, the Son and the holy Spirit, *God* in his life of intimate personal love. The redemptive mysteries of Christ's life have a trinitarian form – our salvation is from the Father through the Son and is completed in the sending of the holy Spirit by the glorified Son. The dialogue of Father and Son which is the Paschal mystery, is completed in that further revelation and in that sending of God's Personal Love i.e. the holy Spirit which we term the mystery of Pentecost. The Trinitarian mystery itself is revealed and actualized in our world and in our history for no other reason than that man may enter into personal communion of life with the Father, the Son and the holy Spirit. The establishing of an abiding personal oneness of man and God is the single purpose of everything that God has done for man.

The oneness of God and man finds its supreme instance in Jesus Christ. He is the foundation and the exemplar of every grace relationship. Every man who stands in grace does so through Christ and in Christ. The incarnation is the grace relationship *par excellence*: it is the means and the model of our being-in-grace. Our grace relationship is patterned after Christ's; but it cannot be set on the same level as his for

Christ is unique. Our oneness with God in grace can be compared even if from a great distance, to Christ's oneness with God. There is a real analogy here. Our personal relationship to God is in some way like Christ's relationship. And this personal oneness with God which we possess is the deepest meaning of the word "grace".

The Reformation Conflict about Grace

Grace was one of the main issues, if not *the* central issue which the Council of Trent discussed. The Council saw that its main work was the clarifying of the traditional faith of the Church in the light of the new understanding of this faith proposed by Luther and the other Reformers.

Luther's theology of grace began as an attempt to restore what he conceived to be the biblical understanding of grace to its properly central position. The validity and Catholicity of some of his early insights is beyond question. He was doing nothing more than recalling the Schoolmen of his day to the more traditional path. This intention was undoubtedly the mainspring of his earliest writings. He attacked his contemporaries, the late Scholastics, because he saw them as neo-Pelagians; men who had destroyed the essential note of grace itself – that it is and remains a gift of God to man.

Luther, however, himself an Augustinian friar, seems to have been influenced by the darker stream of Augustinian theology represented by such thinkers as Gregory of Rimini. Added to this his own personal spiritual struggles seem to have confirmed him in a pessimistic view of man. He understood and interpreted his personal spiritual experience in terms of the darker theses on fallen man and his sinfulness which he read in the more pessimistic stream of Augustinian theology.

The seeds were already there in the Catholic Luther for the developed anthropology or doctrine of man which the theologians of the Reform produced. Luther himself never systematized his original insights, though he did radicalize his position sharply under attack from Catholic theologians.

This process of radicalization is accurately described as a Protestantization of his original Catholic insights. The *sola* fides, *sola* gratia, *sola* scriptura complex was only gradually built up although by the time of Trent, 1545, what had been initially with Luther an attempt to reintroduce certain emphases into the Catholic tradition had become manifest heresy. There had emerged a recognizably new understanding of man and God in which the emphases of Luther had been radicalized and systematized as the basic truths about personal salvation – their balancing truths or emphases being left out of consideration as non-essential. This Reformation anthropology was categorically rejected by Trent which specifically condemned any teaching which alleged a total corruption or destruction of man's nature as a result of sin. Trent reaffirmed very strongly the fact that fallen man is not substantially impaired in his basic human qualities.

Trent

Trent on grace can only be fully understood when seen as a reaction. The Council Fathers were concerned first of all to preserve man as man, as the starting-point of Christ's salvation. Trent reaffirmed that after the fall man remained fully man, pitiably weakened it is true, but essentially unimpaired. Defending man's integral humanity after the fall Trent was equally adamant that this weakened, but not corrupted nature, was totally transformable and was in fact really, truly and internally transformed by the justifying grace of Christ. So it set itself to reject firmly the Reformers' contention that justification was imputed and external and not real or internal. For the Reformers sinful man remained radically unaltered after justification. Justification meant that God did not take account of his sinfulness any more. Trent categorically denied this position and heavily emphasized that grace meant ontological transformation, new being, new life, a re-creation, a renewing of man in the image of the Trinity, which justified and sanctified him, transforming him really and internally.

Given the Reformers' teaching on fallen nature and grace we can understand the reason why Trent was very much preoccupied with the reality of created grace. It was obliged, in fact, to leave on one side for the moment other facets of the doctrine in order to meet this precise challenge. A quotation from Trent on grace – its description of justification – indicates this: 'Justification', it says, 'is not only the remission of sin, but the making holy and the inward renewal of man through the voluntary acceptance of grace and the gifts in which a man from being unjust becomes just and from being an enemy becomes a friend, an heir, according to the hope of eternal life.' And further 'We are renewed in the spirit of our minds and are not only reputed to be, but are called, and really are, just, receiving in us each one his justice according to that measure which the holy Spirit gives, according also to each one's disposition and co-operation.' (D 799). We see all through the passage an insistence on the reality of the change effected in man by grace, but there is no reference whatever here to the much more fundamental and traditional understanding of grace as in the first place the living and personal presence of the Divine Persons.

The Heritage of Trent

The Tridentine preoccupation with created grace has persisted in our Catholic theology of grace until very recently and has dominated the presentation of the teaching on grace in the manuals of theology. Van Noort's *De Gratia* illustrates this point well. He gathers his material under three major headings – the Process of Justification, Habitual or Sanctifying Grace and the Virtues and Gifts. Out of sixty-five pages dealing with justification, sanctifying grace and the gifts which accompany it, only two pages are devoted to the indwelling Trinity. It is strange in fact that Van Noort refers to this indwelling presence as the 'crown and peakpoint of all justification' but does not go on to investigate or analyse it as grace. The created effect of God's presence – sanctifying

grace – is analysed in great detail, but not its more fundamental cause – God himself mysteriously present to the soul.
This facet of grace remains unexamined. Van Noort is taken
as only one example from among the manualists, there are
many others who could be cited too.

Scriptural Perspectives on Grace

When we turn from our current manuals of theology to
Scripture we find a different emphasis in the presentation
of grace. In Scripture, grace is above all else a personal
presence of God to the justified sinner.

a) *The Pauline Writings.* For St Paul grace or man's
sanctification is first and foremost a being brought within
the realm of the Spirit; it is a definitive removal from the
realm of the flesh by a communication of the personal Spirit
of God.

In the Pauline concept 'spirit' or '*pneuma*', the personal
Spirit (*Pneuma*) of God, is the central and commanding
element. All other significations of 'spirit' or '*pneuma*' in
St Paul are secondary and derived from this primary one.
Every created grace, every way of 'being in the Spirit' to
use a Pauline expression, every way of being spiritual or
'*pneumatikos*' is a consequence and a manifestation of the
personal presence of the Spirit. For Paul we have our
'*pneumatic*' or 'spiritual' being (i.e. created grace or our new
being) precisely because we have received the personal
Spirit or *Pneuma* of God. This new life of ours is the out-
growth of the personal Spirit's personal presence, the
necessary echo in our created existence of God's creative
voice – which is himself. All 'spiritual' existence appears as
an effect of the possession of the uncreated Grace, the Spirit.
God's presence, the Spirit who is given to us, is the cause
of our new existence and explains everything else. There
is a great emphasis in Paul on this aspect of our salvation.

Speaking to his Christians whom Paul describes as
enjoying a 'life in the Spirit', he says in Romans 8:9:

You are not in the flesh, you are in the Spirit, if the Spirit of God really dwells in you. Anyone who does not have the Spirit of Christ does not belong to him. But if Christ is in you, although your bodies are dead because of sin, your spirits are alive because of righteousness. If the Spirit of him who raised Jesus from the dead dwells in you, he who raised Christ Jesus from the dead will give life to your mortal bodies also through his Spirit who dwells in you.

In the epistle to the Ephesians 1:13 we find Christians described as 'sealed with the promised Spirit'. This figure of the seal and the impression in wax is rooted in Scripture. It is taken up and used again and again in the Greek Fathers, who developed the theology of the indwelling Spirit.

b) Johannine Writings. The Johannine writings, on the other hand, describe grace as life, grace as being generated by God, grace as being in God, grace as being in Christ, as being in the truth, as being in love, as being in the life, as being in the possession of God's seed or God's anointing, thus placing the created aspect of grace well in the foreground. This emphasis on the created aspect of grace, however, never obscures the more significant fact of the inner indwelling of the Spirit. Even when we find the created aspect of grace given prominence of St John's thinking we are always aware that this created aspect which he expresses as life, or light, or being in the truth and so on, is the result of a personal presence of God to the believer. The writings of St John are full of allusions to *this abiding presence of God in the man who possesses grace.* For example, in the eucharistic discourse Christ says: 'He who eats my flesh and drinks my blood abides in me and I in him' (*John* 6:56). More striking again are Christ's words: 'I will not leave you desolate, I will come to you: yet a little while and the world will see me no more, but you will see me because I live as you will live also, and in that day you will know that *I am in the Father* and *you in me* and *I in you*' (*John* 14:18–20). The

reference to the vine and the branches is also very significant:
'Abide in me and I in you. I am the vine, he *who abides in
me* and *I in him*, he it is that bears much fruit' (*John* 15:5).
Again Christ says: 'I have made known to them thy name
and I will make it known that the love with which thou hast
loved me may be in them and *I in them*' (*John* 17:26).

In addition to speaking about the abiding presence of
Christ in those who love him and whom he loves, John's
writing speaks very clearly about *the Father and the Son
together* making their dwelling in us. 'If any man loves me he
will keep my word and my Father will love him, and *we
will come to him and make our home with him*' (*John* 14:23).

There is reference in John also to the presence of the
Spirit who is given to us and abides in us. This is a frequent
theme of the Johannine writings. Christ says 'I will pray
the Father and he will give you another Counsellor to be
with you for ever, even the Spirit of Truth whom the world
cannot receive because it neither sees him nor knows him,
but you know him *because he lives in you and will be in you*'
(John 14:16–17).

These separate references to Christ's presence, to the
Father's presence and to the Spirit's presence, are clear.
Now more significantly still if we take John, Chapter 14,
we can see that in this particular chapter the references to
the presence of the Spirit, of Christ and of the Father are
part of a pattern. In this chapter John speaks first of all,
i.e. from verses 15 to 17, of a presence of the Spirit, then
immediately following he speaks of a presence of Jesus in
verses 18–22. Then directly after that he speaks of a presence
of the Father: – ' "I will pray the Father and he will give
you another Counsellor to be with you forever (16), even
the Spirit of truth whom the world cannot receive because
it neither sees him nor knows him. You know him because
he dwells with you and will be in you (17). I will not leave
you desolate; I will come to you (18). Yet a little while and
the world will see me no more, but you will see me; because
I live, you will live also (19). In that day you will know that

I am in my Father and you in me and I in you (20). He who has my commandments and keeps them; he it is who loves me; and he who loves me will be loved by my Father and I will love him and manifest myself to him" (21). Judas (not Iscariot) said to him: "Lord, how is it you will manifest yourself to us and not to the world?" (22) Jesus answered him: "If a man loves me, he will keep my word and my Father will love him and we will come to him and make our home with him." ' (23).

It is clear then that for John the Christian is brought into the closest personal intimacy of life with the Father, the son and Spirit. The new life of the Christian is a sharing in the divine life. As the divine persons mutually live in one another in their mysterious oneness of divine life and nature, in an analogous way they live in the Christian and he lives in them. The Christian is drawn into the Trinity, to live as son of the Father, to participate in the Son's sonship, to be in the Spirit.

The Fathers, especially the Greek Fathers, place great emphasis on grace as the personal presence of God. For these Fathers, God's presence is an effective presence marking man. A most striking figure or metaphor which they use is the metaphor of the seal and the impression it makes on the wax. The seal is the divine presence of the Trinity, even the divine Spirit himself, who divinizes man. St Basil and St Cyril of Alexandria are outstanding examples of this type of Trinitarian theology of grace.

Grace is Fundamentally God Himself Given to us

Scripture and the Fathers remind us that the basic truth which we must clearly set out in our theology of grace is that what God gives us, what we mean essentially and fundamentally by grace, is God himself, and not just created gifts – as wonderful as these are. The divine intention is to bring us into personal union with God, with the three Divine Persons. As this union cannot involve any change in God there must be therefore a change in us to make it possible.

I

This change is created grace. But essentially and above all grace is God communicated to us in the mysterious reality of his tri-personal life and love.

When we look at grace in this way we realize that the divine presence, the gift of himself, is what God means us to have, and that this is the core of our grace life. Everything else is there only as necessary to the achievement of this divine communication. Grace, as God's gift of himself can only be understood at the deepest level in the light of John's words: 'God is love'. There is no explanation or reason for this gift of himself other than God's own love.

The God of whom we speak as love, who gives himself to us as grace, is not a unipersonal God. There is within him an inner communication of being, of life, of love, for he is a Trinity, and it is as a Trinity that he gives himself. The communication of himself which we call grace is a reflection of, and a mysterious continuation and projection of, that divine life and love which is the life of the Trinity. For there is within God himself a self-giving.

God the Father is the principle, or starting-point of the divine life and love. God the Son is the image, the perfect expression of this divine life and love, and God the holy Spirit is the mutual gift of Father and Son that completes the self-giving which is the divine life. It is these three living and loving persons who invite us to share their life, to enter into a personal communion with them. It seems clear then that grace, which is radically divine life communicated to man, remains the life of the Trinity. Grace, therefore, for us means fundamentally our being established in a personal relationship to the divine persons, to each of the divine persons, to the Father, to the Son and to the holy Spirit.

We encounter the three divine persons and we are joined to each of them in a real relationship. Our union is not a union with God as one, but with God as three-in-one. Our union is not personal or hypostatic as Christ's is but it is much more than an external association with the one God.

Our union with the Trinity in grace participates in some
minimal degree in the closeness of its model which is the
hypostatic union. Like that union of humanity to the Son of
God it does not in any sense offend against God's unity.
Our existence as sons of the Father in the Son and in the
Spirit; the fact that the Trinity lives its trinitarian life in
us and with us; that we are drawn into the communion of
life and love which God has in himself – these are deeply
mysterious truths, but they are the hard facts of our existence
as Christians and they are also the deepest meaning of the
word 'grace'.

Pastoral Comment

Is the Trinity absent from people's spiritual lives? Are
many Catholics almost instinctively involved in what Karl
Rahner terms 'a kind of pre-Christian monotheism?' And
has most of the preaching they have heard been preoccupied
with preserving the oneness of God even, it seems, at the cost
of obscuring in practice the real distinction of persons? Is
this preaching itself controlled by an inadequate manualist
theology which does scant justice to the data of Scripture or
the Fathers, particularly the Greeks, on this point?

I believe we must answer 'yes' to every question in the
previous paragraph. And that we must determine to change
the situation.

We must take courage from the modes of speech we find
in Scripture and in the Fathers. There is no doubt at all
that in the New Testament and in writers like Basil and
Cyril of Alexandria we find a certain healthy freedom of
expression we will not find in our cramped manualist
presentations. When Scripture speaks of God as our Father,
it is the Father of Our Lord Jesus Christ who is meant. There
is no fear apparent that such a manner of speaking may
mislead us into believing there are three Gods. Likewise
Scripture and the Greek Fathers emphasize very plainly
that the holy Spirit dwells in us in a particular and proper
way – again it seems without fear of misleading anyone.

Our preaching on grace should, it seems plain, concentrate itself on presenting grace in trinitarian and personalist terms and we should realize that in speaking freely of the wonders of the trinitarian personal life into which we are drawn the Scriptures themselves and the greatest Christian writers call us back to a certain Christian freedom of expression in expounding this most profound mystery to God's people.

Conscience:
The Guidance of the Spirit

ENDA McDONAGH

God's self-communication in Christ is visibly and tangibly continued for man in a community and demands a community response. The Christian revelation, in continuity with the earlier stages of God's self-giving to man in the revelation to Israel, is a community reality. It can be accepted, understood and lived only in community. And it is of itself directed to the formation of a community, the kingdom to which all men are summoned to be the sons (and daughters) of the Father and brothers (and sisters) of one another.

The current preoccupation with the community character of Christianity as evident, for example, in many of the developments of Vatican II, does not conflict with the personal character of the relationship between God and the individual human being. In fact the very opposite is true. Person and community are correlative terms and inter-dependent realities. The life and growth of the one is bound up with the life and growth of the other.

The relationship between God and the individual, based on God's self-giving to that human person, has just been discussed under what is technically known as grace. It is the business of this chapter to consider some of the implications for living of this individual relationship. The term 'grace' stresses the gift-character of the relationship between God and the individual. It is indeed a gift of God. In fact as has been stated so often, it is God's gift of himself out of love that establishes this relationship. The obvious implication of grace for living then would seem to be one of gratitude on the part of the recipient, the individual human being. And it would be possible and useful to discuss the whole Christian life and each action in it in terms of giving thanks. So that each truly Christian action would be an expression of thanks to the Father in Christ by the power of the Spirit. And this would be one way of illuminating the connection between Christian living and Christian liturgy.

Faith

The theme of this paper is somewhat different as it takes up the human reaction to God's self-giving at a stage presupposed in the act of thanksgiving, the stage of recognizing God in his self-giving, the stage of faith. Without faith it is impossible to please (*Heb.* 11:6), to thank God or indeed to have any personal relationship with him. Faith is in the words of the Council of Trent 'radix et fundamentum omnis justificationis' (DS 1532) the root and foundation of that transformation of man by God's self-giving which is called justification. The follow-through of this initial reaction, personal recognition of God as he gives himself to man, constitutes Christian living. It is in the most literal sense a life of faith.

To be capable of responding to God's offer of a relationship, man must at least in a general sense be a relational being. That is, he must through self-consciousness be able to distinguish himself and others, and, in the course of this distinguishing or recognizing, take possession of himself (in varying degrees) and entrust himself to others (also in varying degrees). This is sometimes expressed in short-hand by saying that he must have intellect and free will or be able to know and be free to choose. And it is a correct way of describing the reality as far as it goes. However it makes too sharp a distinction between intellect and will, knowing and choosing, as if knowing were not intimately influenced by choosing and not merely choosing by knowing. The inbuilt capacity and drive to know is of course governed by how we choose to use and develop it.

In addition the presentation in terms of intellect and will does not highlight the personal character of the knowledge and choice involved in a relationship, does not point out that it is another person that is known and chosen, not some object or action. And the effective knowledge and choice of the other, which really constitute an entrusting of self to the other, depend on and at the same time influence the knowledge and choice of self in self-possession and self-acceptance. To give self to another in a relationship one must obviously be able to know that other in a personal way, as the term of the gift. In that same act however there must be some knowledge and some possession of the self that is given. Self-possession and self-giving go hand-in-hand and mutually influence one another. As he is a material and historical being, man's knowledge and possession of himself, his recognition of any other and self-gift to him can be achieved only through history, in time. His self-knowledge, self-possession and self-gift remain continuing tasks. Human relationships are always in the making.

This is the being addressed by God, to whom God reveals or gives himself in search of a personal relationship. The initiative rests with God and if he did not care to seek such a relationship man would not be able to make the first move. It is then a grace or gift but exceeding the element of gift in human relationships to the extent that the divine exceeds the human. In a human relationship the initiator, if he can be distinguished, offers himself, one human being to another. In the 'grace' relationship God, divine being, offers himself to a human being. If a human relationship is to develop, the initial offer must be understood by the other. The two concerned must in the broadest sense of the term speak the same

language, so that the one recognizes the other as offering or
responding. This is always possible between normal adult
human beings as they can find some means of communicating at least in intelligible gestures. As between God and the
human being a wholly new problem arises, which again can
only be solved by God, the initiator. He must use some signs
intelligible to the human, belonging to man's world therefore
but which can be understood by man as communicating a
different and divine world.

The human capacity to know, to recognize and accept
another person as communicating himself is not sufficient
of itself to recognizing and accepting the divine self-
communication. In communicating himself to man and
through the human world in which man lives, God must at
the same time enable man to recognize in a personal way the
God who transcends this world, to recognize, accept and
respond. For such recognition is not any intellectual awareness of some impersonal power above, beyond or in any other
prepositional relation to this world. It is the recognition of a
personal being offering himself in a personal relationship
which would draw man out of himself and at the same time
fulfil him in a way exceeding any human fulfilment which he
knows.

Recognition of God in his self-giving, where that recognition is the genuine personal going out of oneself to know
and accept the other as he is, is what is called faith. And
both in its divine 'object' and its human subjective grasp
of that 'object' it is a gift from God to man.

The personal response of faith as recognition of God in
his self-giving has an inherent dynamism. It does not observe
and record the presence of God as one might observe and
record the presence of a mountain or a tree. Recognition of
the other as a person implies a personal commitment which
is missing from the observation of a tree or a mountain. It
establishes, or at least initiates, a bond of union or community with that person which commits one to value and
serve him as he is. Personal recognition is the beginning of

love. Of itself it tends towards that union we call love – at
different levels and in varying degrees. Where the person
recognized is divine the commitment implied has the most
far-reaching consequences. It implies in fact a whole way
of life which is a way of love and of growth in love. To know
God, to recognize him as he offers himself to man, in
particular in Jesus Christ, this is the meaning of life. And
to know God truly is to love him, for he is love.

On insisting that faith is a personal recognition, awareness
by the human person of God as personal, I wish to emphasize
its fundamental characteristics as initiating a personal
relationship. Undoubtedly this knowing God in faith must
include some knowledge about him. To know somebody
always includes knowing about him – something of the
kind of person that he is. And this something will be formulated in various concepts and propositions. To know
about him however, to have such formulated concepts and
propositions, as one has for instance about Napoleon or
St Patrick, does not necessarily involve knowing him.

So it is with faith and God. By faith one knows him and
at the same time one knows about him. There are concepts
and propositions which describe him in his self-giving to
man, as he reveals himself in his dealings with man. Because
these dealings took a definite historical shape, because of
man's historical nature, they are known as 'Salvation
History'. The content of 'Salvation History' forms the content
of our faith, what we know *about* God. This content is not
of course a static formula but a living message which is
always capable of further penetration or more precise and
relevant formulation by the living, knowing community of
the faithful. But faith terminates not in such formulations
but in the personal God.

The full elaboration of the relation between knowing God
and knowing about God is not necessary here. Two further
points may be mentioned.

What is known about God as personal in his self-giving to
man emerges in the New Testament as the startling truth

that he is the one and only God of Abraham, Isaac and
Moses and yet that he is tripersonal, three persons in one
God. The trinitarian cast which this gives man's relationships with God has already been discussed. It is a response to
the Father in Jesus Christ, (that is, as sharing his sonship)
by the power of the Spirit. It is the gift of the Spirit promised
by Jesus before his return to the Father and sent by him at
Pentecost, that enables man to share the divine sonship of
the second person. By the Spirit he is able to say Abba,
Father, to personally recognize God in his self-giving. This
recognition (faith) is a gift, more precisely the gift of the
Spirit, or the transforming effect on man of the divine self-
giving which as it impinges on man is seen to be that mutual,
personal gift of Father and Son which in the mystery called
God constitutes the person known from the New Testament
as the Spirit. Faith is a gift of the Spirit. It is the Spirit
enlightening man and enabling him to recognize with Christ
the Father as Father. This enlightening and empowering role
of the Spirit has important implications for the fuller
understanding and implementing of the life of faith.

A second point in the relation between knowing God and
knowing about God, and one relevant to a discussion about
morality as the expression in action of faith arises in considering the living and morality of those people who do not
know about God, at least as he has explicitly revealed himself
in Jesus Christ. Can they have faith? And if not, does what is
to be said here about Christian moral activity as the expression and development of faith as man's initial response to
God, have no relevance for them?

It is not possible here to deal fully with all the implications
of this problem. In brief, it may be said that all men are in
the same actual situation in relation to God. They are called
to the same destiny, union with the Father in Christ as sons
and brothers. This destiny has been achieved for them in
Christ. The call is theirs as members of the race
redeemed by Christ, of which he is the new head, the new
Adam. They can however recognize and interpret it only

in terms available to them in the society in which they live. For many this will rule out, *a priori*, an explicit Christian interpretation.

These too, however, in seeking to come to terms with themselves, their lives, their neighbours, will encounter the challenge to move out of themselves, to seek the truth, to accept other moral values, to love others for their own sake. This may or may not take a religious form. It may or may not be very articulate. But each man is faced in his own way with the mystery of life (and death). That mystery is ultimately the mystery of God. The call in whatever fashion to face that mystery, to move out of or transcend himself, to entrust himself to truth, goodness, love, is the call of faith. And it will be realized or made concrete in the moral decisions or actions of day-to-day living. From the Christian point of view the mystery of God in Christ is only implicitly encountered and inadequately grasped in its basic reality. But the reality is present to each man and cannot be evaded.

Conscience

Man's recognition of the divine call in faith, whether explicitly as in the Christian believer or implicitly, incompletely, as in religious or non-religious acceptance of the challenge of transcendence, provides the true framework for human living. This basic recognition, or refusal to recognize, is not something that happens once for all. It gradually emerges in the life of the individual through the multifarious major and minor decisions he has to take, the major and minor challenges he has to accept or reject as he grows up. Each challenge is an invitation from God speaking to him in a particular situation, an invitation to express his recognition of and response to God as Father more fully. To do this he has to understand the invitation as precisely as he can. He must make sure of what exactly God is asking of him, what exactly recognizing the Father and behaving as a son involves here and now. He must seek, in the accepted phrase, to form a correct conscience judgement.

His conscience judgement then is his reading of the invitation issuing from God in the actual situation in which man finds himself. It is his basic recognition of God taking its particular shape in the here and now. It is faith in the concrete. It follows then, that to act against the careful findings of one's conscience judgement in a particular situation or to refuse to investigate the meaning of a particular invitation is to fail in that basic recognition of God called faith. It is to sin. Whatever is not of faith is a sin, says St Paul. For him, who in fact gave the Christian Church the term conscience and its first developed understanding, faith and conscience are inextricably related. The one determines the general position of the Christian, the other his particular realization of this in an individual situation.

What is demanded then is a correct understanding of God as he gives or reveals himself in each particular moral situation. This understanding emerging in the human mind expresses itself in will or in action. Good moral activity is doing the truth, where the truth is ultimately God's self-giving as invitation to man. Good moral activity is again knowing the one true God, the expression in action of this recognition. Bad moral activity is deliberate failure to know the one true God, the creation instead of false gods to be served for one's own satisfaction. Sin, as the Old Testament records, is a form of idolatry.

The understanding of morality as doing the truth properly underlines a man's commitment to seeking the truth in his individual situation. The first stage of realizing man's response to God is the effort to understand what God is asking of him here and now. To fail to make this effort is to fail at the very first stage of response. And it may well be that most human failures occur just at this point. So many of us fail to do that which we ought to do because we deliberately ignore the real situation confronting us. We pass by on the other side, overlooking all those whose needs are no less obvious than the man robbed on the way to Jericho. We never knew 'it was like that' is the constant cry of all of us when suddenly we are faced with some monumental evidence of our neglect. 'When did we neglect you hungry or thirsty, sick or in prison' proves no excuse in the presence of Christ (*Matt.* 25). An implicit and sophisticated 'I'm all right Jack' allows one to enjoy the extra comfort of not knowing the real sufferings of one's neighbour, and the consequent demands of knowing the one true God. Failure to be genuinely aware of these needs in every society today, as well as in the general human society to which all belong, is a failure in faith, a form of implicit idolatry or even atheism. A god of one's own comfort and satisfaction, a no-god has been substituted for the one true God of Jesus Christ.

The first demand of the divine invitation then is to know the situation, to seek to understand as fully as possible what God is asking here and now. In the hitherto accepted terminology this was described as the obligation to inform one's conscience. Unwillingness to do this, to use the best available resources to understand the truth of the moral situation facing one, is already an unwillingness to respond to the one true God. This unwillingness may show itself in ignoring the 'physical' facts of the situation as it were, the 'physical' facts of hunger, of physical, emotional or mental illness, of loneliness and homelessness, of lack of educational opportunity, of prison conditions, of war, of corruption in politics, etc., etc., or the 'moral' implications of any of these – my capacity and obligation to do something about these as an individual and as a member of society.

Knowledge of the 'physical facts' and of their 'moral implications' cannot be achieved by the individual person simply on his own. Like any other knowledge it is a personal achievement in community. The resources of the community are available and necessary to each man in understanding the demands of his moral situation, in informing his conscience. Without the accumulating factual knowledge of the scientific and wider human community he could not hope to have any adequate grasp of the facts of his situation. Without the accumulating moral wisdom of the community, with its continued analysis of the moral implications of these facts, he would not be able to analyse his own situation.

Authoritative Teaching and Individual Response

To know the one true God in a particular moral situation and to do that truth, involves more knowledge about God and about the moral implications for man of his self-giving. Knowledge about him and about these moral implications has always accompanied his self-giving in the Judaeo-Christian revelation. The climax of the self-giving in Jesus Christ naturally included the climax in knowledge about God and about responding to him. The understanding of both these continues to develop in the community in which that self-giving in Christ is perceptibly and historically present and to which Christ promised the gift of the Spirit in pursuit of these truths. It continues in the Church.

For the Christian believer the Church as the perceptible locus of God's self-giving in Christ, and the community in which the knowledge about him resides and develops, offers indispensable guidance in his search to understand the demands of his own situation. The moral teaching of the Church, that teaching which issued from its knowledge of and reflection on the revelation made in Jesus Christ, forms a primary source of the Christian's conscience judgement. Recognition of the one true God of Jesus Christ in any situation will incorporate the authentic knowledge about him and his moral demands which form the heritage of the Christian Church.

As far as moral direction is concerned, such teaching is not to be regarded as primarily legal in form and imposed on the person and his situation from the outside. It is in fact a reading from within of the God-man relationship established in Christ, of the elementary demands of that relationship, of the basic directions in which it must develop. These demands or directions are intrinsic to each relationship and become urgent or obligatory in the different situations of each man's life. So recognizing God in faith (doing the

truth) and responding to him personally (expressing love
or charity) involves certain elementary demands such as
worship (and hence avoidance of blasphemy), respect for
the life of one's neighbour (and avoidance of murder), truth-
ful communications with one's neighbour (and avoidance of
lying). These are intrinsic to the relationship established by
God between himself and man and between man and man.
They emerge from the two-fold dynamism of that relationship expressed in the New Testament as love of God and love
of neighbour.

In identifying such intrinsic elements in the Christian
situation in general, Christian moral teaching remains at a
rather general level. This does not make it irrelevant or
dispensable. Both positively and negatively it enables the
individual Christian to understand the basic structure of his
invitation. But the Christian himself must give precise shape
and substance to that structure, so that the expression of
his faith or love, in truth-telling, in respect for his neighbour's
life, etc., will achieve myriad different forms in accordance
with the myriad different situations of myriad different
people. There is a genuinely creative element in moral
decision and moral action which should not be obscured by
such decision and action in terms of applying and fulfilling
a law. Personal relationships can never be properly expressed
as conformity to a law. To run one's friendships or marital
relationships in accordance with a legal complex on the
model of the bye-laws of a railway would destroy the very
relationship itself, removing all spontaneity, creativity,
genuine personal love. Yet one must be aware of and respect
the underlying structure of the relationship if it is to grow
through the spontaneity and creativity and love. Awareness
of the underlying structure is more important at the
beginning or when the relationship is weak or going through
some crisis. It enables one to avoid very bad mistakes, or at
least to recognize them and seek to repair them. In a healthily
developing relationship these underlying structures, safely
incorporated with one's basic attitude of love, no longer

obtrude, and the demands of the relationship are met
spontaneously, lovingly, and creatively. This applies no
less to the God-man relationship than to the man-man
relationship.

In forming his conscience-judgement the individual
Christian will use all the resources available to him, in
particular the moral teaching of the Church. He will however
be aware of its general character and not stop short at considering its negative direction only. Avoidance or inaction
is not in itself an expression of love. The understanding
and expression of this teaching will also vary from age to
age as man's general or social situation develops. So the more
general directives about respect for life and its relation to
war, for example, or capital punishment, may develop considerably from the condition of primitive tribal living to
the situation today. Similarly the directives about the use
of property must develop very radically. Such development
does not invalidate earlier understanding as appropriate to
its own time although the understanding at any particular
time may well be defective, and to that extent inappropriate,
on account of man's inherent weakness. And in this development not only are the official teachers involved, the bishops
and the theologians, but also the whole Christian community,
and not in isolation but as part of the wider human community. The human community as a whole is as we have
seen, involved in the same situation or relationship with God.
The inability of many to recognize this in explicit terms does
not mean that they cannot, in grappling as they must with
their own situation, develop an understanding of the
demands of their situation (and so of their relationship with
God and with one another) which coincides with or even
exceeds the understanding of Christians at particular points.

The history of human morality and of human moral
reflection testifies to the capacity and achievement of the
human community as a whole in understanding the moral
implications of human living. This moral wisdom of the
race is of course also available to Christians. And in con-

tinuing dialogue with it they may develop and enlarge their own moral understanding.

Because his conscience judgement is the first stage in his response to God in any situation, the individual is obliged to listen to God as carefully as he can. He must use all the resources available to him to understand what God is saying as fully as possible. For the Christian this includes the moral understanding and teaching of the Church. And precisely because it is the first stage in his response to God, the individual has to make this judgement or decision himself about what God demands of him. He cannot have his conscience judgement made for him by others. The moral guidance which is available to him in the community, Christian or general, may outline authentically and authoritatively (in the case of the Church) the basic structure of the demand, but his judgement, while incorporating this, must be his own personal assessment of the demands of truth and love in each particular case. To remove from the individual this personal assessment would be to rob his response of its dynamic, creative and genuine love quality, as if a man could only make love responses in accordance with a detailed recipe. The intrinsic structure of his situation and its demands can only be generally described in the moral teaching of the community. To force it into detail is to falsify it as well as to deprive the individual of his right and obligation to make his own assessment.

Understanding the Church's moral guidance in this general way is not to deny its authority or its *general* applicability. It is not to yield to the fashion which would make every situation so unique that it has nothing in common with other apparently similar situations so that general moral principles or values do not enter intrinsically into the situation. It is not to yield to situation ethics as propounded by Fletcher and others.

It is however to recognize the limitations of this general guidance even when it is formulated in the most accurate way for men of our time. It must not be used as a substitute

K

for, but as a guide to and support for personal judgement.
And it should not be thought of primarily in legal terms
akin to human laws, as it frequently is, so that the personal
judgement is simply an application of the law to the particular situation. The general teaching has some of the aspects
of law, and it can be formulated as prescribing either
positively 'you must respect human life' or negatively 'you
must not kill'. But neither of these, even if they are further
qualified, always provides a sufficient guide for a man's
obligation to respect for human life, which must obviously
go far beyond the prohibition of direct killing of the innocent.
What are the obligations, for example, of an individual in
face of famine in his own country or abroad? Here the call
to respect human life has infinitely varying meanings for
the different individuals in their different situations. To do
nothing to kill these people directly is clearly not an adequate
answer to this call.

The creative dynamic character then of the moral decision
and consequent response cannot be reduced to application
of law, least of all of prohibitions. The intrinsic structure of
the God-man and man-man relationship which can be
discerned and formulated should be incorporated either
implicitly or explicitly into the judgement and response. For
the Christian, the Church has a special role in discerning
and formulating this structure. But its formulation is general,
always in need of further development, and may and should
learn from the moral wisdom of the race. The Spirit which
was given to the Church at Pentecost is at work also in the
race as a whole and available to the individual as he searches
out the demands of God in his situation.

The recognition of God and his demands in a particular
situation is no more a purely intellectual exercise than is that
basic personal awareness of him called faith. It involves
intellectual activity and knowledge about God and his
demands. But as pointed out earlier, ability to recognize the
demands of love in a relationship grows with the love and
depends less and less on explicit advertence to the knowledge

about the other or about the basic structure of the relationship. Sensitivity to the demands of God and one's neighbour
in any situation depends on the state of the relationship, so
that the holier, more loving person has a more sensitive
conscience. This may well make mistakes and it can never
ignore or contradict the basic structure of the relationship.
But growth in true Christian charity frees a man from the
cruder mistakes of others, so that he no longer sees the basic
structure as confining or limiting in the way a person with a
less developed relationship would.

Freedom

To exercise his creative (i.e. loving) capacity in recognizing
the demands of the situation and in responding to it, the
individual Christian needs room to manoeuvre; to transform
the general moral directives of the Church into a detailed
plan of life is not only to falsify these directives but to deprive
the individual of his right and obligation to creativity and
to growth. To insist on such detailed planning by human law
for priests, religious or lay-folk is again to falsify the genuine
notion of human law as general prescriptions for the common
good and to confine in strait-jackets people with the right
and obligation to find in the general context of their lives
the best way for them to respond to God and their neighbour.
Freedom, not only psychological, but social, freedom in
society, in the community of the Church, is essential to
Christian response. Without freedom it is impossible to
please God.

The Declaration of Vatican II on Religious Freedom
reasserted the genuine Catholic tradition in a developed
way that had been resisted by many Catholic thinkers and
churchmen in the last hundred years, and that depended on
insights gained to some extent outside and even in spite of
the Church. As a statement of the freedom of the individual
in civil society to seek the truth about God and to live in
accordance with it as he knows it, it is excellent. It does not
deal however with the freedom at issue here – the freedom

necessary within the Church to allow the individual to
respond as freely and as fully as possible to God and his
neighbour, as a result of the faith brought to him and
nourished by the community of the Church. To develop
that faith in his personal way by his understanding and living
of it, he needs of course guidance and protection so that he
may understand what has been called the basic structure of
the relation to God and his neighbour, made available to
him in his Church. But he needs increasingly freedom, with
the risks it involves, if he is to move out of the infantile
stage of being led by the hand and so scarcely making a
personal response at all, to the adult stage of following Christ
out of personal conviction and in a developing way. For the
sake of its members (i.e. of itself) the Catholic Church has to
ensure adequate social freedom, including the freedom to
make mistakes. And this must pervade the Church at every
level, universal, regional and diocesan, parochial and
religious house. Without such social freedom Christians
cannot attain the perfection to which they are called.
To deprive them of that opportunity is an awesome
responsibility.

This is not to deny the need for some law for the ordering
of the community at large, to ensure the possibility of
exercise of freedom. But such a law should be at a minimum
in the Church of Christ. And of course with the diminution
of law personal responsibility is increased, the opportunity
for personal response is increased. And this in itself is a good,
a God-given good, even if the possibility of personal failure
is also increased. To say otherwise would be logically to
maintain that God made a mistake in creating men to be
free. It would also be to ignore the redemptive situation in
which we live, where the Spirit speaks to, guides and sustains
free (but only free) if fallen men.

Freedom, in the sense of social freedom, as the necessary
accompaniment of psychological freedom, is not to be
presented as simply an end in itself. It is the necessary state
in which a man becomes human and Christian, in which he

attains that maturity in relation to God and his neighbour, described in the New Testament as the freedom of the sons of God. This freedom is like all Christian realities a gift (of the Spirit) and a task (of the individual). It is achieved by the progressive liberation of the individual from his inhuman and self-centred tendencies, so that gradually taking fuller possession of himself and his energies, he is able to devote them unselfishly to the love and service of God and his neighbour. For the freed, liberated son of the Father, the response of love is spontaneous, sustained and all-enveloping. Such freedom is attainable only in part and gradually in this life. It is constantly threatened by selfishness and the self-deception that invokes. Yet it is a distinguishing characteristic of the gift of the Spirit in these last days to the community of the faithful. The community of the faithful is the community of the explicitly liberated. Its claim and its preaching to the world is to be such. This liberation remains the gift of the Spirit. It cannot be commanded. But it presupposes for its reception and exercise psychological and social freedom. The Church has ever been a tenacious defender of the first. Today more attention to the second would make its claims in the name of Christ and his Spirit more credible. To allow its own members to develop and to fulfil its mission to the world, the Church should appear more clearly at this social level as an area of freedom.

Liturgy:
The Whole Christ mediates with the Father

Kevin McNamara

The present chapter, which deals with the Church's Liturgy, is closely linked to the chapter on the Church. There we saw how the Church came into being as the world-wide community of those who, through word and sacrament, share in the fruits of Christ's reconciling work. Our purpose now is to examine more closely how this sharing takes place, to enquire how individual men and women, by freely co-operating with God's plan, make their own the salvation won by Christ. It is principally in the Liturgy that this happens. It happens, of course, in other ways also. The Church is also sanctifying men in extra-liturgical activities, e.g. preaching, catechetics, the teaching of the Magisterium, pastoral letters, the care of souls in its many forms, the prayers and sacrifices of the faithful. All these, however, culminate in the Liturgy. In the Liturgy the Paschal mystery itself is continually made present in the world. It is therefore the point on which the entire mission of the Church converges and the source from which, ultimately, it draws its energy and life. It is primarily in the Liturgy that the '*admirabile commercium*', the wonderful interchange, between God and man takes place, God graciously giving himself to man and enabling man in turn to give himself to God.

Israel's Sacred Rites: their Twofold Purpose

Like the Church itself, the Liturgy has its roots in the Old Testament. Already in Israel we find certain public acts of worship appointed by God for his people: sacrifices, blessings, prayers, purifications, ritual actions of various kinds. In these rites, which reached their climax in the festivals celebrated at intervals throughout the year, the bonds of unity between God and his people, as well as among the people themselves, were expressed and developed in a special way. In them the people gave expression to their dependence on God, acknowledging in a spirit of filial love and obedience that he was their Saviour and the source of their existence as a people. In addition, they experienced his saving power, for in and through the cult God was acting to purify and strengthen his people. Israel's cult must not be seen, therefore, simply as the fulfilment of a religious obligation on man's part. It was also God's gracious gift to man. In it he acted powerfully to draw man into closer union with himself. Indeed it was only because of this gracious divine initiative that Israel's worship could find favour with God.

This two fold purpose of Israel's ritual or, as it is usually called, liturgical activity, is seen most clearly in the act of sacrifice. At all times in human history man has chosen sacrifice as the most appropriate act of religious homage, and it was in keeping with this universal instinct that God appointed sacrifice as the principal liturgical act of his chosen people. Sacrifice has been understood differently by different peoples, but the idea that it is an act of homage is universal. Essentially, sacrifice is the dedication to God, the solemn making over to him for his exclusive use, of some valued possession. In some more or less corrupt forms of religion, sacrifice is seen as a way of providing food for a god, or the idea is found that food offered in sacrifice is thereby imbued with the life of the god, which is then shared by the worshippers in partaking of the sacrificial food. In higher forms of religion the true significance of sacrifice is more in evidence. Sacrifice appears as a gift offered to God in order to express man's recognition of his dependence on God for his life and for all he possesses. Coupled with this motive of adoration other, related motives are found: petition, thanksgiving, atonement for sin.

It is this latter understanding of sacrifice that is found in Israel. Yahweh, the God of Israel, made use of sacrifice, the spontaneous expression of man's submission to God, in order to develop and keep alive the spirit of humility, penance, confidence and fidelity which was the very heart of Old Testament religion. In the Jewish sacrifices sometimes one, sometimes another motive was uppermost in the minds of the worshippers. But whatever the dominant motive – thanksgiving, petition, atonement for sin or simple recognition of God's excellence – in God's eyes the basic function of every sacrifice was to express and promote the recognition by Israel of its complete dependence on him. This was true not only of sacrifice, but also of the other ritual acts, to which reference has been made above.[1]

The Cult, Culmination of God's Service

This understanding of Israel's cult immediately creates a link with its wider service of God. Fundamentally, the purpose of the cult was no different from that of the observance of God's law in the ethical and general religious spheres. Morally good conduct and fidelity to the general demands of the covenant were also significant only in so far as they expressed a right interior attitude towards Yahweh. In the concrete circumstances of human life the exact discipline imposed by such behaviour was a most effective guarantee of sincere acceptance of Yahweh's rule. Its influence was constant and all-pervasive, and affected every member of God's people. Nevertheless, the cult had its own special contribution to make. In it the people expressed their relationship to God in an intensified and formal way. Here

---

[1]Cf. R. de Vaux, *Ancient Israel. Its Life and Institutions*, London 1961,451. ff

they solemnly reaffirmed their day to day recognition of dependence on Yahweh and gave it a new impetus for the future. It was by no means, therefore, an isolated element in Israel's life. It had meaning only through its continuity with what went on before and after it. Properly understood, it was the moment when the abiding covenant relationship between God and his people was most fully realized, the central point of reference for a people whose whole existence was bound up with fidelity to God's word.

Israel's service of Yahweh had two complementary purposes: the expression and formation of a right disposition in the worshipper, and the giving of glory to God. This was true of both forms of service, the general service of a holy life and the special service of the liturgy. The two purposes of this comprehensive service were mutually complementary; in fact, they were no more than two aspects of the one activity, two sides of the same coin. In forming in himself a right disposition of mind the Israelite was also giving glory to God; for this disposition consisted essentially in the recognition of God's excellence. It was this two fold programme that a group of shepherds near Bethlehem were to hear proclaimed by heavenly voices on the occasion of the birth of the Saviour: 'Glory to God in the highest and on earth peace among men with whom he is pleased.'[2] God's glory and the formation of a right disposition in men's hearts go hand in hand. They are in fact mutually interdependent. Moreover, the use of the rich biblical idea of peace, with its suggestion of order, well-being, true contentment, brings out the fact that it is in recognizing God's rule and thereby giving him glory, that man achieves his own happiness. Man, in other words, is never more truly himself than when he goes beyond himself and places all his reliance on God. The liturgy of Israel was designed to impress forcibly upon man, and give him a unique opportunity of affirming in personal action, this complex, but at the same time, simple message.

---

[2]*Luke* 2:14.

In this lay the fundamental importance of the liturgy in the life of Israel.

Sacred Time: the Festivals

The peculiar efficacy of the cult was bound up with a number of factors. In common with religious peoples in every age the Israelites believed that at certain times in the course of the year their God made himself particularly accessible. These times were therefore sacred. This was the origin of the various holy days and festivals that played so important a role in Israel's life.[3] The religious year revolved around three great festivals: the combined feast of Passover and Unleavened Bread, celebrated in the early spring; the feast of Weeks, so called because it fell seven weeks – more precisely, fifty days – after the Sabbath immediately following the Passover; and the great harvest feast known as the feast of Booths or Tabernacles. All three feasts had their roots in primitive agricultural or nomadic celebrations. The Passover can be traced back to the magical rite, common among camp-dwelling peoples, of sprinkling the pegs of their tents with the blood of a slaughtered lamb in order to ward off threatening disaster. After the Israelite occupation of Canaan we find a feast possessing obvious links with such a Passover rite – the term 'Passover' referred to the harmless passing of the evil that had threatened – in close association with the agricultural feast of the Unleavened Bread, which celebrated the havesting of the first sheaves of barley. The name of the latter feast was derived from the flat cakes eaten on the occasion – there was as yet no new leaven, and the leaven of the old year could no longer be used. The feast of Weeks, too, like that of Unleavened Bread, was originally a corn festival; it celebrated the end of the wheat harvest, which in Palestine was in the third month of the year, roughly corresponding to our present month of May. The third great feast of the year occurred in the seventh month – in the present

[3]See the excellent study, to which I am much indebted: Thierry Maertens, *A Feast in Honour of Yahweh*, London 1967.

September – and had its historical roots in the celebration of the successful conclusion of the grape harvest. It was marked by great rejoicing which went on for several days, during which the people lived in temporary dwellings. This custom, which gave its name to the festival – the feast of Tents – had its origins in the practice of the primitive grape gatherers, in order to expedite the work of the harvest, of living in huts made from branches of trees and erected in the open fields.

All these feasts, then, were ultimately pagan in origin. Nevertheless, it is essential to note that they received a completely new meaning among the Israelites. Instead of being magical and agricultural rites, bound up with pagan superstitions and nature worship, they came to be associated with the saving intervention of the living God in the history of his chosen people. The Passover – or Pasch – was linked to the preservation of Israel from the plague of the slaughter of the first-born of the Egyptians by the angel of Yahweh: in executing judgement God mercifully 'passed over' his own people. The accompanying Feast of Unleavened Bread recalls the rapid flight from Egypt which followed, when there was no time to prepare ordinary bread. The feast of Weeks also received a completely new significance. It became an official commemoration of the giving of the Law to Moses by Yahweh on Mount Sinai, an event which, according to Jewish tradition, took place fifty days after the escape from Egypt and the first Pasch. A similar 're-reading' took place in regard to the feast of Tabernacles. Here too a new interpretation arose in which, once again, historical events replaced the rhythms of nature and God's gracious initiative in favour of his people wrested the primacy from man's efforts at propitiation. The motif of the tents, from which this feast took its name, was now linked to the wanderings of Israel in the desert, and the whole feast became an exultant expression of thanksgiving for what God had done for his people in leading them through the desert to take possession of the land he had prepared for them.

During the celebration of these feasts the Israelites believed

that they were particularly close to God. The religious
concept of sacred time was here powerfully operative. Not
merely did the feast call to mind in a most vivid way God's
mighty deeds of salvation on behalf of his people in past
times. This in itself created a powerful religious atmosphere
and aroused fervent feelings of awe and gratitude. But the
true concept of the feast went much further. Essential to it
was the still more dynamic idea that God was here and now
re-enacting among his people what he had done for them in
the historical intervention that was being commemorated.
The individual Israelite taking part in the feast was exhorted
to realize that he himself was the beneficiary of God's saving
act, that God was now doing for him what he had done in
former times for the people as a whole: rescuing him from
his enemies (Passover), proclaiming the law for his acceptance (Weeks), leading him safely through the vicissitudes of
his journey through life (Tents).

Corresponding to this salvific aspect of the festival, which
emphasized God's merciful initiative, was the attitude of
soul demanded of the worshipper. It was necessary that he
should align himself with the spirit of the feast, opening his
heart to those sentiments of thanksgiving, homage and
repentance which the commemoration of the divine intervention called forth. By making these attitudes his own he
gave acceptable worship to God. He went away from the
feast having faithfully rendered the service demanded of
him, and with the assurance of God's blessing for the future.
Even in this aspect of the cult, however, although man's
contribution finds its appropriate place, the divine action
retains the initiative. The interior attitude demanded of man
was itself the gift of God, something to be humbly asked for
and gratefully received.[4] Nowhere more strikingly than in
this profound recognition of God's sovereignty and man's
utter dependence is the difference between Hebrew and
pagan religion revealed.

---

[4] Cf. *Ps.* 51:10; *Ezek.* 36:26.

All that has been said in regard to the Israelite feasts applies in some measure also to the weekly Sabbath. The Sabbath was a day of freedom and rest, reminding the Israelite of God's mercy in freeing him from slavery and from the power of his enemies, and in granting him a settled home in Canaan at the end of the desert wanderings. It was closely associated too with the Israelite's understanding of God: it called to mind God's creative activity and his lordship over nature, as well as his loving mercy in setting man free from labour on this day each week, a blessing which, over and above its primary significance, pointed beyond itself to the final and complete rest of the coming messianic time. The Sabbath was therefore a day in which God drew near to his people. On this day sacrifices were prescribed and all were exhorted to give special attention to that holiness of life which was the constant demand of Yahweh from his people. Once again we see the fundamental principle of the cult at work: the cult represents a time of particularly intense devotion to God, a constantly recurring high point in that life of service of God to which the Israelite people was called.

Sacred Sites

In addition to this concept of sacred time another influential idea was at work in the cult. The Israelites believed, and here again they were at one with religious peoples throughout the world, that there were certain places with which God had associated himself in a special way.[5] After the occupation of Canaan we find several local shrines – those at Shiloh and Mizpah won particular prominence – throughout the country where festivals were held and sacrifices offered. These shrines had been erected at places where Yahweh was believed to have manifested himself, thereby indicating that worship in such places would be pleasing to him. This system of local shrines,

---

[5] Cf. W. Eichrodt, *Theology of the Old Testament*, Vol. I, London 1961, 102-7.

though it had the merit of making participation in the cult easily available throughout the land, had nevertheless its disadvantages. It was of the essence of the Israelite faith, with its paramount stress on the divine transcendence, that God could not be circumscribed in any place or shrine. This principle was in constant danger of being forgotten, not least because of the influence of the surrounding pagan shrines, and only the greatest vigilance on the part of the religious leaders succeeded in upholding it. Eventually it became necessary to unify worship: after the exile sacrifice was offered no more at local shrines but only in the temple at Jerusalem. This ensured that the faith of Israel would escape the two fold danger inherent in the cult – the reduction of God to human proportions by tying his presence too closely to a particular place, and, as a corollary of this, the fragmentation of the one God of Israel into a number of local deities. The temple worship, for all its stress on the holiness of the temple and on God's presence therein, was careful to avoid any suggestion of a limitation of God's being or activity. The dominant idea was that the temple was the place where God manifested himself rather than, properly speaking, dwelt. From time to time he showed himself in the sanctuary, though only under the veil of his 'glory', the cloud which was the visible sign of his presence. In general, however, his relationship to the temple simply meant that he was accessible through the temple worship, that this was the place appointed by him for that intimate meeting with himself which was realized and expressed in the cult.

By thus keeping at bay the threat to divine transcendence involved in the concept of the sacred site, Israel was able to profit from the powerful stimulus to worship which this concept provided. In association with the idea of sacred time, of which the calendar of festivals was the institutional expression, it helped to arouse the liveliest feelings of God's presence and to assure the worshippers of his gracious dispositions with regard to them. It is the fervent wish of the devout Israelite to be present continually in the temple:

'One thing have I asked of the Lord, that will I seek after; that I may dwell in the house of the Lord all the days of my life, to behold the beauty of the Lord, and to enquire in his temple.'[6] Place, time, historic associations, the prayers and actions of the cult – all combined to call forth homage, reverence, repentance and gratitude. On the one hand, these dispositions, in the intense degree in which they were evoked by the cult, were the supreme expression of Israel's loving service of its God; on the other hand, they were themselves the choicest gift of God to his people, for only God could create in man the 'right heart' which was the very soul of worship, and the cult was the principal means by which he brought this effect about.

The Definitive Festive Assembly

Another aspect of the cult should be mentioned briefly. Not only did it recall, and make a present reality for the worshippers, God's saving action in the past; it also aroused hopes of a new and definitive divine intervention in the future. God had not yet given the messianic blessings in their fulness. A day would come when he would dwell among his people in a way previously unknown.[7] On that day he would be immeasurably closer to them than he had been even in the time of the desert wanderings, which always remained fixed in the national memory as a time of God's special nearness to his people. The feasts were therefore occasions of renewed hope and of fervent longing for the messianic times. When the people assembled at Jerusalem to celebrate the feasts, their reunion brought to mind the day when not only the entire nation, the twelve tribes of Israel, but all the nations of the earth would gather around Mount Sion to worship the one God and be joined to him in a holy fellowship. Here we find the historical roots of the eschatological dynamism, the straining after Christ's Second Coming,

---

[6]*Ps.* 27:4.
[7]*Zech.* 14:16, etc. Cf. *Apoc.* 7:9-17. See Maertens, *op. cit.*, 92-4, 243 f.

that was later to be an important feature of the Christian
Liturgy.

Israel a Priestly People

To sum up the results of the rapid study of the cult we have
just made we may say that the cult was God's gift to his people.
In and through it God forged closer bonds with his chosen
people. Through it their allegiance to him was continually
renewed and the inner attitude of soul which gives meaning
and value to religion was created, developed or restored.
At the same time the cult maintained and strengthened the
unity of the people itself. The frequent coming together
which the celebration of the feasts required renewed its
consciousness of being a single people. The historical
associations of the feasts also worked to produce this effect.
The worshippers were vividly reminded of the events to
which they owed both their origin as a people and the
successful acquisition of the land in which they dwelt. The
feasts were thus a re-living of the high points in the people's
history. They were so many channels by which its traditions
and ethos were handed on and absorbed.

The role of the cult in the life of Israel may be expressed
in terms of priesthood. Israel as a whole was a priestly
people. 'You shall be to me a kingdom of priests and a holy
people.'[8] Basically priesthood connotes special access to
God, both for oneself and on behalf of others. As the
'pontifex' or bridge-maker, the priest establishes union
between God and man – and thereby among men themselves.
Israel was a priestly people inasmuch as it had been consecrated to God and called to enter into a special relationship
with him on behalf of the whole world. Another way of
looking at the same truth is to say that Israel was called to a
sacrificial life. Sacrifice and priesthood are co-relative: as a
'kingdom of priests' Israel was appointed to offer sacrifice.
This meant living a sacrificial life, for sacrifice was meant to

---

[8] *Exod.* 19:6.

be an expression of interior homage and dedication, with the self-abnegation and goodwill towards one's neighbour which this attitude of soul demanded. In was in this inner disposition, this turning to God in penance, obedience and love, which was at the same time a turning of every Israelite towards his fellows, that the true meaning of the priestly and sacrificial role of Israel consisted. This point is made with all desirable clarity by the prophet Amos, who, in Yahweh's name, condemns sacrifice that is but an empty external rite:

> I hate, I despise your feasts, and I take no delight in your solemn assemblies. Even though you offer me your burnt offerings and cereal offerings, I will not accept them, and the peace offerings of your fatted beasts I will not look upon. Take away from me the noise of your songs; to the melody of your harps I will not listen .But let justice roll down like waters and righteousness like an ever-flowing stream.[9]

What God wants is interior fidelity to himself and to the twofold precept of the Law, and external sacrifices are of value only in so far as they give expression to this attitude. That is why every good action could qualify as a sacrifice in a wide sense: as a genuine expression of devotion to God it fulfilled the basic purpose of sacrifice. Thanksgiving, for example, is a sacrifice: 'He who brings thanksgiving as his sacrifice honours me.'[10] Almsgiving too is an agreeable sacrifice, as is every genuine religious act. Of course sacrifice – and priesthood – is to be found in a special way in the official cult. Nevertheless, in a wider, but true sense, all Israel is a priestly and sacrificial people, and every moment of its life is claimed by God as the expression of its priestly service.

Jesus Christ the True Priest

Israel's role in God's plan was essentially preparatory. Its liturgy therefore, like every aspect of its life, looks to the

---

[9]*Amos.* 5:21-4.
[10]*Ps.* 50:23.

L

future. It finds its true meaning in the priesthood of Christ.
Christ is the great High Priest, the only priest really worthy
of the name. He alone is the effective bond of union between
God and man. In his person God and man are united in the
Son of God incarnate. No closer association of human and
divine is possible. There is in Christ a profound unity of
being, without prejudice to the distinction of natures, and,
in the moral sphere, complete harmony of his divine and
human wills. His entire life and work were devoted to
realizing to the full the implications of this mysterious unity.
As far as he personally was concerned, this meant living here
below a life of complete fidelity to the Father's will. When
he had travelled the path of obedience and suffering marked
out for him he would pass over into a life of perfect intimacy
with the Father, free from the limitations imposed on him by
the conditions of earthly existence. And at the same moment
he would make this fellowship with the Father freely
available to all mankind.

The Cross was the decisive act by which all this was
achieved. In the Cross Jesus summed up the entire course of
his life. It was the act appointed for him by the Father as
the supreme expression of his loving obedience as eternal
Son. Here he achieved the highest exercise of his priesthood,
entering into complete and definitive union with God as
representative Head of the human race. Henceforward all
who wished to achieve intimacy with God had only to unite
themselves to the loving act of self-surrender which
constituted Christ's sacrifice on the Cross. A new Liturgy had
now been established. Through it were realized the two great
ends to which the liturgy of Israel had been directed from
the beginning: the giving of glory to God and the creation of
a right heart in man. Israel's liturgy had been true and
efficacious only because it foreshadowed the Liturgy of
Christ. All future Liturgy too would derive its meaning from
the same source. Christ's sacrifice alone was acceptable to
God, and the only possible justification for any further
liturgical worship would be to enable men to participate in

that priestly act of Christ. Through such participation they would be able to render God acceptable service and, in so doing, to share in God's gift of himself which was fully made to man in the resurrection of Jesus from the dead.

The worship of Israel was built around the concepts of sacred rites, sacred times, and sacred places. All three concepts reach fulfilment and a new level of significance in the death and resurrection of Christ. In this event their purpose is achieved. Christ's sacrifice on Calvary is the sacred rite *par excellence*. It speaks eloquently of man's complete acceptance of God's rule, which is the genuine meaning of religion. On the other hand, it witnesses to God's love for man in giving his Son for man's salvation and, in the resurrection, raising up mankind together with him to a life of intimate fellowship with the Blessed Trinity. In this raising up of Jesus as a source of new life for the human race, we see fulfilled the aim which had motivated the Old Testament sacrifices.

This aim had found expression particularly in the sacrificial meal. In this meal the victim of sacrifice, already accepted by God and now being partaken of by the worshippers, was considered to be a bond of union between the two sides – though the underlying idea here, it should be noted, was the fellowship traditionally associated with a meal, not the pagan concept of a magical force communicated to the gift offered in sacrifice whereby the worshippers could share in the life of their god.[11] The risen Lord, the victim who truly finds acceptance with God, becomes the real, eternal bond of union between God and those who accept Jesus in faith. And it is once again in the form of a sacrificial meal – the eating of the sacrament of Christ's body – that this unity is to be fully established. For the future liturgical rites will be legitimate and efficacious only in so far as their aim is to unite men with the Paschal mystery, the death and resurrection of Jesus. For in that event the purpose of all sacred

---

[11]Cf. de Vaux, *op. cit.*, 453.

rites and feasts is fulfilled. The object of these had always
been the expression and development of an inner attitude of
submission to God. In Christ's Paschal mystery this attitude
is found in a supreme and perfect degree. All future rites
therefore will have to be related to this event. And the
principal rite of the new covenant will accordingly be that
celebration – the sacrament-sacrifice of the Eucharist –
which makes the Paschal mystery actually present to men
and enables them to enter fully into it.

In the Paschal mystery too the true sacred time has come.
This is the moment in history when God gives himself fully
and definitively to man in a holy union. From now on all
sacred time must be consciously referred to this time. It is
valid only as a time in which this time is somehow recaptured.
That is why Easter is the greatest Christian feast. It is pre-
eminently our sacred time because it is entirely directed to
evoking the resurrection event and making it a present
reality enfolding and re-making the worshippers. For a
similar reason every Sunday of the year is a great Christian
feast – greater, it must be said, than our liturgical practice
has always recognized. Sunday is the day on which the
Lord rose. For every Christian it is a special occasion for
union with him in his definitive triumph over death. And
this occasion presents itself most perfectly at Mass, which
represents a special concentration of the sacred time of
Sunday. At Mass, through the power of the Spirit, the time of
Christ's Paschal mystery effectively becomes present time
for the Christian assembly. Here the closest possible union
with the self-sacrificing, victorious love of Christ on Calvary
is placed within our reach.

Finally, in the death and resurrection of Jesus the concept
of sacred space acquires a new meaning. This may be
summed up in the statement that Christ is the true temple.
The Old Testament temple, we have seen, was the place in
which God showed himself and made himself accessible to
his people. But this temple was but a prefiguration of Christ.
It is in Christ that God truly reveals and gives himself to

man. In St John's Gospel we read of Christ discussing the glories of the Jewish temple with the Pharisees. 'Destroy this temple', Jesus said, 'and in three days I will raise it up.'[12] And John immediately adds: 'But he spoke of the temple of his body.'[13] He spoke, that is, of his own person as the place where fellowship between God and man was to be realized. In the risen Lord the knowledge and love of God had been fully given to a member of our race, and it is by joining ourselves to him that we can share in this relationship. The idea of sacred space is here transformed. It is realized now on a wholly personal plane. No longer is a site or building thought to be the meeting-place *par excellence* of God and man. The community itself is now revealed as God's true abode on earth. Taking possession of this community in its inmost being, he transforms it and sets up within and with it an unceasing interchange of love and knowledge. What we saw to be true of sacred rites and sacred time in the Christian dispensation applies here also. Henceforward material temples and shrines can be no more than images of the true temple which is Christ's body, and the means by which this body may develop and express itself. Even in Old Testament times, indeed, the true purpose of sacred sites had been to promote interior unity between God and his people. But it is only in the light of Christ and his Paschal mystery that man has been able to understand the full significance of this unity as willed by God. More fundamentally, it is only in dependence on Christ's work that this unity has at all times been possible, whether in the preparatory and inchoate fashion of the Old Testament period, or in its full realization in the times ushered in by the coming of Christ.

Sharing in Christ's Priesthood

As the one Priest of the new and eternal covenant, Christ is the sole means of access to the Father. In order that others

---
[12] *John* 2:19.
[13] *John* 2:21.

too may be able to reach the Father Christ gives them a share
in his priesthood. He has committed his priesthood to the
Church in such a way that baptism, which admits a man
to the Church, gives access to Christ's priesthood also. St
Peter testifies eloquently to this participation by the
Christian in the priesthood of Christ and describes the dignity
of the Christian life which rests on it.

> Come to him, to that living stone, rejected by men but
> in God's sight chosen and precious; and like living stones
> be yourselves built into a spiritual house, to be a holy
> priesthood, to offer spiritual sacrifices acceptable to God
> through Jesus Christ. . . . But you are a chosen race, a
> royal priesthood, a holy nation, God's own people, that
> you may declare the wonderful deeds of him who called
> you out of darkness into his marvellous light. Once you
> were no people but now you are God's people; once you
> had not received mercy but now you have received
> mercy.[14]

Here the ideas of priesthood and temple are interwoven.
Because Christians, through their union with Christ, are a
holy priesthood, they thereby constitute a 'spiritual house'.
Their incorporation into Christ, the true Priest, makes of
them the true temple. Together with him and through him
they have intimate access to God, offering him acceptable
worship and receiving those divine favours which are at once
the condition for and the fruit of such worship.

The Christian exercises his priesthood in various ways.
These may be summed up under two headings: the priesthood of a holy life and the priesthood of the Liturgy –
though these, it should be noted, do not constitute two
distinct titles to priesthood, but are rather different mani-
festations of the Christian's incorporation into Christ in
which essentially his priesthood consists. There are a number
of New Testament texts which bring out clearly that through

---

[14] *Pet.* 2:5, 9 f.

grace and charity we can perform holy actions which, though not sacrifices in the narrower sense, are nevertheless true sacrifices, genuine priestly acts. They are not acts of public ritual; yet they effectively express and develop the Christian's union with God. In the passage from 1 Peter quoted above we find reference to the 'spiritual sacrifices acceptable to God through Jesus Christ', which are offered by the Christian. Elsewhere in the New Testament these sacrifices are named in detail. In the epistle to the Hebrews we read: 'Through him then let us continually offer up a sacrifice of praise to God, that is, the fruit of lips that acknowledge his name. Do not neglect to do good and to share what you have for such sacrifices are pleasing to God.'[15] Praise of God, thanksgiving, good works in general – these are the sacrifices of the Christian. We find the same teaching in the epistle to the Philippians, where St Paul, referring to the gifts which he has received from the Philippians, writes: 'I have received full payment and more. I am filled, having received from Epaphroditus the gifts you sent, a fragrant offering, a sacrifice acceptable and pleasing to God.'[16] The generosity of the Philippians is here described as a sacrifice. In its full range, however, the sacrificial worship expected of the Christian embraces his whole life, as the following passage from the epistle to the Romans makes clear: 'I appeal to you therefore, brethren, by the mercies of God, to present your bodies as a living sacrifice, holy and acceptable to God, which is your spiritual worship.'[17] It is his own person that the Christian must offer in sacrifice, in other words his entire life and activity.

This teaching was to become a central and frequent theme in the writings of the Fathers. It provides the background to the famous definition of sacrifice formulated by St Augustine, who is particularly eloquent on the dignity conferred on the Christian through his union with Christ

[15]*Heb.* 13:15f.
[16]*Phil.* 4:18.
[17]*Rom.* 12:1.

the Priest: 'Every work tending to effect our beatitude by a holy union with God is a true sacrifice.'[18] Because the life of grace puts the Christian on terms of intimacy with God, every good action he performs becomes a new bond of union with him in whose service it is performed.

On the other hand, a Christian exercises his priesthood through the official Liturgy of the Church. By the Liturgy is meant the continual realization in the Church, under the form of visible signs, of the reconciliation of mankind with God effected by Christ on the Cross. Christ himself has entrusted this system of signs to the Church. Moreover, it is he, present in the Church through his holy Spirit, who gives it life and power. Through the Liturgy the Church perpetuates on earth the priestly activity of Christ until his Second Coming. Essential to the Liturgy is the idea of order, of a definite system arranged by authority. It is Christ and, within limits, the Church, who appoint the forms of liturgical activity in the Church. Christ has instituted the sacramental system, which is the centre of the Liturgy and is itself centred in the Eucharist. On the other hand, the Church is responsible for many of the rites and ceremonies in which the sacraments have come to be expressed – only the 'substance' or essence of the sacraments stems from Christ. From the Church too come the Office, the sacramentals and the ordering of the liturgical year, all institutions appointed by her for the more effective sharing by the faithful in the priestly work of Christ.[19]

In this description of the Liturgy two points deserve particular attention. The first is that the Liturgy does not denote simply, or even principally, rites and ceremonies, though these are essential to it. The Liturgy is primarily a sacred event, the actualization in the Church of Christ's priestly function. As such, it is effected by the holy Spirit, the Spirit of Christ. Corresponding to what we have seen of

---

[18]*City of God*, 10, 6.
[19]Cf. E. J. Lengeling, 'Liturgie' in H. Fries (ed.), *Handbuch der theologischen Grundbegriffe*, Vol. II, Munich 1963, 86 ff.

the Old Testament liturgy, the Liturgy of the Church has two aspects: on the one hand a descending movement consisting in the sanctification of the worshippers by God, an aspect which is particularly evident in the sacraments; on the other hand, an ascending movement, whereby the worshippers express their homage and dependence, an aspect which is more obvious in the eucharistic sacrifice and the Sacred Office. Both elements are nevertheless to be found in the entire Liturgy. Though one may predominate, it still remains true that in the sanctification of men God is glorified and, on the other hand, in giving worship to God men are made holy. In the twofold process at work here lies the real significance of the Liturgy – the creation of an interpersonal communion in which man shares in the life of the Godhead.

It is through the sacramental characters of baptism and confirmation that the Christian is given a share in the Church's Liturgy. The life of grace equips him for the priesthood of a holy life, the characters for the priesthood of the Liturgy. The baptismal character is an initial consecration of the Christian to the official worship of the Church; it deputes him to receive the other sacraments and to take part in the eucharistic sacrifice. This initial consecration is ratified and finally stabilized by the character of confirmation: the confirmed Christian is definitively consecrated to the holy Spirit and his mission, and takes his part in the Liturgy as a fully-fledged member of the worshipping community.

Unity of the Christian Priesthood

As in the Old Testament, the Liturgy of Christ's Church is intimately linked with the Christian life as a whole. This is simply another way of expressing the basic unity, already stressed, of the two forms of priesthood possessed by the Christian, the priesthood of a holy life and that of sacramental worship. The priesthood of a holy life reaches its climax in the blessed Eucharist and, more generally, in the

Liturgy as a whole. In the Liturgy the climax is reached of that attitude of filial submission to God which gives meaning to the 'spiritual sacrifices' of a holy life. Here the Christian's service of God is raised to its highest point, as God reaches down through the activity of Christ the High Priest, and the sacramental sign which carries it, to lay hold of the worshipper and bring to a new level of perfection the religious dispositions with which he has come to worship. On the other hand, it is from the Liturgy, under its twofold form of word and sacrament, that the Christian derives the understanding and strength to meet the challenges of the Christian life. In and through the Liturgy he continually renews his spiritual resources.

There can be no question then of any real opposition between Liturgy and personal devotion. It is in the Liturgy that personal devotion reaches its climax, and if this is not always true at the psychological level, it only underlines the need for a better understanding of the Liturgy. In particular an adequate grasp of the community aspect of religion, of piety as a relationship to God which essentially involves a relationship with one's neighbour, will open the way to a true appreciation of the religious significance of public worship. Another requisite is, of course, an adequate understanding of the liturgical rites. These rites have the character of signs and as such they have a message to convey. Indeed it is precisely in expressing this message – e.g. in baptism, the incorporation of the Christian with the dying and risen Christ – in words and actions that the rite has its sanctifying effect. In order to participate fully in this effect the recipient must have an adequate grasp of what the sign means. Thus equipped, he will discover new depths in liturgical worship and come to experience it as the most satisfying expression of his devotional life. At the same time he will be saved from the error of depreciating personal prayer. This error, though precisely the opposite of neglect of the Liturgy, nevertheless points to a failure to understand it, indeed to the very failure from which neglect of the

Liturgy commonly springs, viz. lack of due appreciation of the inner attitude of soul which the Liturgy is meant to create and express. Where this aspect is given the attention it deserves, it will be clear that private prayer is an essential preparation for the Liturgy as well as a necessary consequence of it. On the one hand it helps to bring about the proper dispositions for genuine liturgical participation; on the other it helps to ensure that what has been done in the Liturgy will be personally appropriated by the individual and put into practice in his life.

The interdependence of life and Liturgy is grounded in the radical unity of the priesthood of the baptized. It is also necessary to stress the close links uniting this priesthood with the priesthood of orders. The ordained priest performs a service for the benefit of the entire community. It is by exercising his priesthood in offering the eucharistic sacrifice and administering the sacraments that he makes possible the priestly activity of lay Christians. Without his office there would be no Liturgy for them to take part in, no vital centre from which to derive the light and strength enabling them to exercise the priesthood of a holy life. Another fact is also evident. It is by exercising his ministerial priesthood that the ordained priest actually fulfils the baptismal priesthood which he too possesses. It is by being faithful to his calling as an ordained minister of the Gospel that he himself grows in personal union with Christ. His special priesthood is set in the wider context of his baptism. There is not therefore a special class of Christians consisting of the clergy, who possess an access to the mystery of Christ that is denied to lay people. The Christian life is the common possession of all the baptized. At every level, even the highest, it is open to the simplest believer. What remains true is that the ordained priest is called to sacred tasks to which others are not, and that these tasks, since they constitute a special call to holiness of life, bring with them the guarantee of generous divine assistance and thereby open the way to intimate union with God.

Despite the different ways in which it is realized in the Church, Christ's priesthood remains one. All Christians are engaged in a common task. In mutual support and dependence they must practise holiness, dedicating their lives without reserve to the loving service of God.

The Eucharist, Centre of the Liturgy

As has been noted more than once in this chapter, the centre of the Liturgy is the Eucharist. Here Christ's Paschal mystery is actually made present in the Church that men may share in it. Nor is it only individuals who benefit. Through the Eucharist the entire Church returns to its origins and is replenished by the redeeming love of Christ which brought it into being. At its heart the Church is a community of love. The Eucharist continually recreates the Church inasmuch as it renews in it that love of Christ from which it lives. The Church has no higher or more vital activity to perform than the celebration of the Eucharist. Here it expresses and develops itself with the maximum intensity. It is by associating himself with this act that the individual Christian renews his Christian existence. At one and the same time he intensifies the bonds uniting him to the Church and is linked more closely to Christ and the Father. This twofold goal he achieves in the highest degree at the moment when he receives the sacrament of Christ's Body. This is the culmination of the eucharistic sacrifice, the means by which its fruits are most abundantly shared by the believer. It is the profoundest source of the unity of the Body of Christ and of the ever-growing incorporation into it of Christ's members.

The very structure of the Eucharist calls attention to this. For in its outward form the Eucharist is a communal celebration. It is a coming together, a visible assembly, culminating in the fellowship of a common meal. As such it is a concentrated expression and realization of the *ekklēsia*, of God's people gathered together by his word. And, like the *ekklēsia* itself, it conforms in its action to the law of

sacramentality. The outer event, in other words, symbolizes
and effects an inner reality. The visible assembly points to
the profound fellowship of minds and hearts in which the
unity of the Mystical Body consists. Moreover, it helps to
bring this fellowship about. For from the beginning it is
orientated to the eucharistic sacrifice and to the culmination
of that sacrifice in Holy Communion, when fellowship
achieves its most intense expression. The actual visible
assembly, being an integral part of the entire celebration,
participates both in the symbolism and in the efficacy of the
action that is performed. Nowhere is the structure and
meaning of the Church more clearly shown forth than in the
eucharistic celebration, and nowhere, accordingly, is the
Church more fully actualized or more powerfully strengthened and renewed. This intimate connection between
Eucharist and Church, which has too long been lost to view,
is today being rediscovered. Its importance for a true
understanding of the Liturgy will be evident from what has
just been said. No less valuable is the contribution it has to
make to ecclesiology. By helping us to see the Church as a
community that is created by the Eucharist and finds its
supreme expression in the fellowship of the eucharistic meal,
it sets the hierarchical structure of the Church in its true
context and calls attention to the primacy of word and
sacrament as the creative sources of the Church's life.

The Eucharist is the centre of the sacramental system.
Alone among the sacraments of the Church, it makes the
Paschal mystery of Christ present among us in its fulness.
The other sacraments too, however, put us in touch with
this mystery. In various ways they make its sanctifying
power present to us. They are Christ meeting us in particular
moments of need and conforming us to himself through signs
suited to our condition. Continuing the incarnational, human
way which God has chosen for his self-disclosure and self-
giving to man, they both reveal and effectively unite us to
Christ, the supreme expression of God's saving love. Like
the Eucharist, however, they do this in and through the

Church. All the sacraments too are actions in which the Church as a whole encounters God. Acted on by the divine power at work in the sacraments, it expresses and realizes its communal life, generating or deepening the life of grace in its members, strengthening and maintaining its structures. The Eucharist, however, remains the focus. The sacraments of baptism, confirmation, penance and orders in different ways prepare the Christian for its celebration; marriage blesses man and wife with a view to giving a new depth and richness to their participation in the Eucharist and to replenishing in due course the ranks of the eucharistic assembly. Anointing of the sick, finally, aims at restoring the invalid to an active role in the eucharistic celebration and at giving him a definitive place in the eternal celebration of praise to which the eucharistic Liturgy looks forward.

The Liturgy and this World

The aim of the Liturgy is to develop Christian life in its fulness. It promotes true interior worship, both personal and communal. Thereby it faithfully reflects the plan by which man fulfils his being: by giving himself to God in and through community life he achieves his true personal development. Ecclesial existence, summed up in sacramental and, above all, eucharistic existence, is the selfless giving of himself by man to others, to God first and then to man, or, rather, first and last to God but to man too inasmuch as he is made in God's image. Here below man lives this life of service in hope of a future consummation. He looks forward to a time when all obstacles to personal union with God will have been completely removed. It is not surprising that this note of eschatological hope is clearly audible in the Liturgy. The heightened fellowship of the liturgical celebration anticipates and points forward to the final union with God at the end of all things. This is the meaning of St Paul's words to the Corinthians: 'For as often as you eat this bread and drink the cup, you proclaim the Lord's death until he comes.'[20]

---

[20] I *Cor.* 11:26.

The same theme is beautifully expressed in the eucharistic prayer preserved in the second century document known as the *Didache* or *Teaching of the Apostles:* 'Remember, O Lord, thy Church, deliver her from all evil, perfect her in thy love, and from the four winds assemble her the sanctified in thy kingdom which thou has prepared for her.'[21]

Meanwhile the Christian remains in the world. From the Liturgy he returns to the daily task from which he has come to worship. Having offered that task to God as the expression of his union with the sacrifice of Christ, he now takes it up once more, strengthened by the grace he has received. Working for God's glory and with the aim of making God's love a living reality around him, not only in personal relationships but also in the structures of society, he brings the world back to God, offering it to him at every moment but especially in the Liturgy. The world remains the world, but is nevertheless consecrated to God. One day, with man himself, it will share in the fulness of salvation which is to be given to creation at the Second Coming. Nothing that man has achieved, or even attempted, in the service of God and his fellowman will be lost. All will endure, only raised up to a higher, altogether new plane, and, together with the praise of the Whole Christ, will play its part in the eternal Liturgy of heaven.

---

[21]*Didache*, 9:4.

Marriage and Celibacy:
Living Christ's Sacrifice

DENIS O'CALLAGHAN

'All of God's people must give testimony to the mystery of
Christ and his kingdom, but this witnessing does not take
the same form for all. The Church leaves to her married
children the function of giving the necessary testimony of a
genuinely and fully Christian married and family life. She
entrusts to her priests the testimony of a life wholly dedicated
to the ever new, absorbing realities of God's kingdom.'[1]

Both marriage and celibacy are Christian responses to
God's invitation to return him love for love in the form of
one's life among men. Although the choice of either one of
these patterns necessarily excludes the other, both options,
inasmuch as they are types of the Christian life, are inspired
by a single ultimate motive, the intent to realize in one's
situation the vocation to which God's love is calling one. In
themselves the options imply quite different emphases.
Marriage is a cosmic reality, it preaches Christ's presence in
the world and proclaims life in the world as a way to God;
celibacy is an eschatological reality, it preaches Christ's
message of a kingdom over and above human experience,
and proclaims that we live our lives in the shadow of
Christian hope. In its way, then, celibacy is the more
radical demand. In human terms it is a privation, it is

---

[1]Paul VI, *Encyclical Letter on Priestly Celibacy*, 24 June 1967, n. 57.

the turning aside from the general way of human happiness and fulfilment, it is the surrender of a way of life to which man is naturally drawn. Unlike marriage, it does not find meaning in itself; it finds meaning only in *being for* something else.

The theology of marriage must be treated at two levels; it has a double core of meaning. As a human event it is part of the order of creation; as a Christian event it is part of the order of redemption. The theology of celibacy is a simpler undertaking. It finds all its meaning in the order of redemption. This itself may give rise to the objection that celibacy ignores the force of creation. But even though Christian celibacy does not find its justification in created reality, this very reality is receptive of the new significance or meaning which celibacy implies. In secular experience people have found celibacy meaningful when it is motivated by the concern to dedicate oneself totally to a particular task. In Christian celibacy this receptivity or openness to meaning places it at the service of preaching the kingdom.

MARRIAGE

Recent years have seen a good deal of writing on the theology of marriage. The overall pattern is outlined in the Constitution of Vatican II, *On the Church in the Modern World*, and theologians have the task of formulating this in more detail. A certain proportion of recent efforts are uneven, in that the approach is prejudiced by concern to support one or other side in the birth-control controversy. It is unfortunate that our theology of marriage should be developing in the shadow of an issue which is really of marginal importance. The debate is absorbing time and energy that could be usefully expended in analysing more fundamental matters.

It is at last agreed that marriage is no longer a matter merely for the canonist. Writing some forty years ago the Dutch theologian, Gerhard van Noort, remarked that in his seminary at Warmund, as in many other places, the course

M

on marriage was confined to the lectures on canon law. In spite of this, it is hardly fair to blame the canonist for taking over marriage. One should blame the theologian, who surrendered his responsibility. The canonist regarded marriage as a contract by which man and woman exchanged perpetual and exclusive sexual rights for the purpose of procreation. In this field he was competent to deal with the nature, purposes, qualities, solemnization and dissolution of this contract. Personal values, love, vocation, spirituality were irrelevant to his task. He felt no need to advert to these and, anyway, they are hardly matters that take easily to codification.

The contract approach to marriage betrays its short-comings, even within the limited field of canon law. The canonist finds himself emphasizing that it is a *special* kind of contract, that it has certain elements, qualities and purposes, which are prior to and independent of the consent of the parties. Implicit in this approach is the notion of marriage as an institution, a complex reality established by divine and human law, which specifies and qualifies the individual contract in that it must be recognized and accepted in the consent of the partners. If this notion had been central and explicit in the canonist's treatment, marriage consent would be described in far more extensive and meaningful terms than the exchange between man and woman of permanent and exclusive sexual rights over one another's body with a view to the performance of acts of a procreative nature.[2] This classical definition of consent makes no mention of partnership, the personal relationship between husband and wife, as an essential purpose of marriage. In confining its interest to biological procreation it does not even give a satisfactory description of parenthood, which is the responsibility not only of producing but of rearing children to maturity.

For purposes of canon law the contract approach may pass

---

[2] C. 1081.

muster, but as a framework for a theology of marriage it is altogether defective. In *Casti Connubii* Pius XI returned to the older system of division provided by St Augustine in his three values of marriage: *bonum prolis* (the procreation and education of children); *bonum fidei* (the fidelity of the partners in a mutual and exclusive love); *bonum sacramenti* (the indissolubility which reflects that of the union between Christ and the Church). Vatican II marks a real step forward in analysing marriage as an institution centred on a community of love between husband and wife. This community of love is the essence of marriage; note how often the Council interchanges 'marriage' and 'community of love', or places them side by side as synonyms for the institution. When one has identified the qualities (permanence and exclusiveness), and the purposes (parenthood and partnership), of this community one has defined marriage. One may now appreciate what Herbert Doms meant when he said that marriage *is* in itself a reality of profound meaning before *being for* something else.[3] For him the love-community or the two-in-oneness of the partners is marriage in its very meaning or essence. At a further stage this dynamic nucleus qualifies, and in turn is qualified by, the essential purposes of marriage.

The Human Institution: Marriage in Creation

Marriage as it comes from the hands of the Creator may be defined as the exclusive and permanent relationship of man and woman in a family unit, or community of love, where new life may be brought to maturity and where the partners may find personal fulfilment.

Man is free to marry or not to marry, but he is not free to decide the kind of marriage which he will have. The pattern of marriage is determined by the Creator, it is independent of man's will and pre-dates any convention entered into by the partners. This pattern is discovered through the experience of man as a bisexual being – male and female, mas-

---

[3] *The Meaning of Marriage*, London 1939, p. 88.

culine and feminine – and by appreciation of the place of marriage and the family in the overall human situation of the person-in-community. The philosophy and theology of marriage develop and become more explicit with the gradual evolution of attitudes and structures in civilization. It is evident that the development cannot take place in a vacuum but must depend to a great extent on what one comes to know of man through sociology, anthropology, phenomenology and psychology. On this level there is the possibility and necessity of dialogue with the humanist.

Then, again, in building up the God-given pattern of marriage man's reason is assisted by revelation. The Old Testament contribution is found not only in the creation accounts of Genesis and in the celebration of human love in the Song of Songs, it is also to be found in the covenant teaching of the prophets (Osee, Jeremiah, Ezechiel, Isaiah) and in the moral attitudes of the wisdom literature (Proverbs, Ben-sirach, Tobias). The marriage teaching of the New Testament is represented chiefly by the Synoptics and by the Pauline epistles.

From the data of human knowledge and experience, and from an analysis of the truths of revelation, we can fill in the pattern of marriage as a secular institution.

Marriage is a community of love. It is not just a juridical bond of contractual rights and obligations. Behind these lies a whole human context which man experiences but does not easily formulate. The heart and soul of this human relationship is love. Law may be interested in the permanence of the marriage bond, but love is concerned with the quality of the partners' life together.

What is love? Love is one of those primitive human experiences which is beyond definition, because there is nothing simpler or more ultimate to provide the terms of a definition. All one can do is describe it. This, too, is difficult, because the very word *love* has been debased in the popular usage which confines it to physical passion or to passing

emotional involvement. Unfortunately, the love of the pop
song stops short at the superficial.

Love is the life of a person in actual community with
another or with others. It may be described as the relation
of one person to another so that they become one in heart and
in mind. Each knows and accepts the other, and this shared
knowledge and acceptance is their life and love together.
This unitive force of love is celebrated by poets and philosophers the world over: 'Union of mind, or in us both one
soul' (Milton). 'Trahit enim amor (quia fortis est ut mors
dilectio – *Song of Songs* 8:6) amantem extra se, et collocat
eum in amato, faciens ei intimissime inhaerere. Plus enim
est anima ubi amat quam ubi animat.'[4]

Friendship and love are fundamentally the same thing,
but in current usage love carries more emotional overtones.
Naturally the quality of love or friendship will depend on the
personalities of the persons involved. Love or friendship is
nothing more than these two persons in relation to one
another; no two relationships are alike. At the same time we
can point out a number of general characteristics which are
common to all genuine friendships or loves.

Love is personal. It joins two persons precisely as persons;
only a person can love, only a person can be loved. This
union of the *I* and the *Thou* in the *We* should be no threat to
the identity of the persons concerned. They may be at one
in having common interests, sentiments, attitudes to life,
and in possessing one another's confidence, but this does not
mean that their separate personalities are blurred. One loves
the other precisely because he or she is singular and unique.
In one and the same relationship love unites and distinguishes. It is as if union and distinction, far from being
mutually exclusive, depend on one another. One might go
further and say that far from being a threat to the persons
concerned, love is a personalizing force, it leads a person to
expand and develop himself. The person is not born full

---

[4]This is from a tract *De adhaerendo Deo* traditionally ascribed to Albert
the Great.

grown; he is constantly in process of becoming, of creating himself. Love provides a climate for this self-realization. One should remark that this personal characteristic of love is evident above all in the love of friendship. This ecstatic love is based on the absolute uniqueness of the other, and its most obvious characteristic is that it is the love of free choice. The personal note takes a rather different form in love conditioned by nature. This cosmic love is based on a common bond between the persons concerned, and it is not a free, a spontaneous response to the other as other. The parent-child relationship is the classical example of this kind of love.

Love is generous. The essence of love is self-gift, a being for the other. Respect, thoughtfulness, consideration for the other are evidence of the presence of love. Exploitation of the other for one's own advancement or pleasure is evidence of its absence. In this way loving differs from liking. If you merely like a person, just as you like a thing, it means that you see him as an object, something there for you. Love is essentially disinterested; it is a gift, not a calculation. Only a person who is secure and self-possessed, who really loves himself, can give himself completely to another in this way. The insecure person will see affection as weakness and love as a threat of domination. Of course, the emphasis on generosity does not mean that one does not intend to gain happiness for oneself in the relationship; it does mean that this happiness is achieved through the other, not at the cost of the other.

Love is total. It is a gift not a loan. Even though a person may realistically foresee that love or friendship may end, it is always permanent in intent. If genuine it sees the other as a person, as a unique individual who is not bound up or absorbed by his situation in space or time. A change in situation may well involve a change in the pattern of friendship, it will not involve a change in its quality.

Love is para-rational. This term is used because love cannot properly be described as either rational or irrational. Ecstatic love is particularly inexplicable to reason.

If one loved someone for his nature, one could explain it, saying that one loved him because he was intelligent, kind, courteous or witty, or because he was like oneself; and if one's love were interested, one could explain it by pointing to what one expected to gain from it – encouragement, relief from loneliness, entertainment or something else. But in fact it is directed to the person, and is disinterested, so that all one says by way of explanation is that one loves the other because he is who he is, and one has met him. After that silence.[5]

This does not mean that love contradicts reason. Fortunately, there is more in man than can be reduced to cold intellectual reason. In a very real sense, from the point of view of reason, love is blind. Love is blind in that it tends to idealize or idolize the other. This blindness is a merciful technique, it filters perception and gives to the experience of love a quality and perfection which almost transcends human nature. Naturally, there is a danger in this. If the blind force of love is allowed to take over it will not survive disillusionment in matters which are really of marginal importance. Therefore, there is a constant need to get to know the other as he or she essentially is. In real life, then, love is always in tension between blindness and clear-sightedness.

Love is creative. Even though love enables the persons involved to realize themselves through their common experience, this does not mean that it closes the persons in on themselves in an autistic union of mutual idolatry. The jealousy which strives to keep the other completely for one's self destroys love at source. Love should not isolate nor insulate people from life, it should free them for life. Love is *sui diffusivum* – it wants to share, to create, to give its own happiness to others.

The above characteristics are found in any genuine friendship. In marriage they are qualified by the fact that married love is essentially sexual. It is the union of man and woman

---

[5]John Cowburn, *Love and the Person*, London 1967, 147.

precisely as male and female, as masculine and feminine. Sexuality colours their whole relationship – spiritual, intellectual, emotional, physical. This sexual love leads to marriage. It is the force which draws man and woman to fuse their lives in partnership. It is sealed in marriage. There it receives the final stamp of exclusiveness and permanence. In marriage 'I love you' means 'I love you alone' and 'I love you always'. Love is often cited as an alibi for divorce and infidelity, but these are really indications of failure in love. Therefore, from the very nature of married love, apart altogether from the more usually emphasized social or legal considerations, the case for a permanent exclusive union can be established.

All love and friendship finds external expression in some act or gesture. The very intimate love of marriage is expressed in the marriage act. This is a sign of the two-in-oneness of the partners. 'The marriage act is in its natural structure a personal act, an act of co-operation, simultaneous and immediate, between the married couple, which by the very nature of the persons concerned and by the character of the act itself expresses the mutual self-gift which, in the words of Scripture, causes them to be united in one flesh.'[6] If this act is to be really an act of love it must begin in the heart and must be marked by mutual respect and consideration. In other words it must be personal. It is exploitation, the very denial of love, to use the other for one's selfish pleasure, *ob solam voluptatem*.

All love is creative, but married love, precisely because it is sexual, is procreative. It welcomes and places itself at the service of new life. The love of the partners is signified in such things as a common name and a life together; it is actually realized in the child. In this sense man and woman become supremely husband and wife when they become father and mother. If the sexual act is the meeting point of their love, a child is the arrival point.

---

[6]Pius XII, *Address to Midwives*, October 1951.

Since marriage founds a family, love in marriage covers a double personal relationship, namely, partnership or the relationship of husband and wife, and parenthood or the relationship of parents and children. This makes family love a composite of what we have called ecstatic and cosmic love.

The nature of the husband-wife relation is discovered from human experience and from revelation. Love in marriage draws husband and wife into a single way of life where they complement one another spiritually and psychologically. The rather barbaric term two-in-oneness is a fair description of the situation. This same unity of soul, mind, and heart is suggested by the biblical term 'one flesh'. Marriage is not just a contract for the performance of sexual acts; it is the common life of two knowing, feeling, living persons, of two persons in love. This idea of complementarity, of companionship of husband and wife, is found in the earlier of the Creation narratives.[7]

The parent-child relation is also essential to marriage. Marriage is for children. It is a vocation to parenthood. 'By their very nature marriage and conjugal love are ordained for the procreation and education of children and find in them their ultimate crown.'[8] The generosity of the parents' love, the total and permanent self-gift of one to the other is realized above all in the child. In the child their love lives. The couple who selfishly exclude a child deny the will to serve new life which is built into their way of life by the Creator. It is true that some couples with the best will in the world do not succeed in their desire to have children. This generous intent in itself purifies their love and saves it from the shallows of selfishness.

The vocation of parenthood aims to produce not just children but mature adults who can take their place in the world. Canon 1013 speaks of the primary purpose of marriage as the procreation and *education* of children. It is now accepted that birth regulation is part of the responsi-

[7]*Gen.* 2:18-24.
[8]Vatican II, *On the Church in the Modern World*, n. 48.

bility of married life, and that biological or random fertility
is an abdication of human reason in this field. Birth regulation is not a lack of generosity or lack of trust in providence.
The whole aim of the parents in their decisions on spacing
and limiting births is to meet their call to serve new life as
generously and as adequately as their circumstances allow.
An appeal to Providence will not justify irresponsible action
in the field of procreation, any more than in any other field.
Men must use the reason and foresight which God has given;
it is presumption to think otherwise.

Marriage in Redemption: the Christian Institution

Between Christians marriage is a sacrament in which
natural wedlock gains a new supernatural meaning, and is
directed to the expansion and the realization of the community of charity. The Council of Trent defined: 'If anyone
shall say that marriage is not truly and properly one of the
seven sacraments of the New Law instituted by Christ, but
that it is a human invention which has crept into the Church
and that it does not confer grace, let him be anathema.'[9]

The recognition of marriage as one of the seven sacraments
was the result of a slow evolution in Church thinking. Even
though many Fathers apply the word *sacramentum* to marriage
it is not to be understood as our technical term sacrament.
It means either that marriage is a symbol of the union of
Christ and the Church, or that it is a sworn commitment to
a way of life. *Sacramentum*, the common word for an oath,
was used to translate the term *mysterium* in Ephesians
5:31.

Some of the Fathers (for example, Origen and Gregory
of Nyssa) were so scandalized by the fact that new life was
procreated through sexual 'concupiscence' that they maintained that if Adam had not sinned God would have established a means of propagating the race more in keeping with
divine and human dignity. In spite of this it was noted that

---

[9]*Denz.* 971.

Christ had blessed with his presence the wedding at Cana, that many of the apostles were married men, and that traditionally in the Church the wedding ceremony implied the blessing of a priest or bishop.

With more profound appreciation of the role of marriage in the Christian life, the theology of the twelfth century admitted that marriage was a sacrament, even if it was a second class sacrament for some of the earlier scholastics. Peter Lombard claimed that the grace conferred by it was a kind of actual grace to remedy the defects of sin, but St Thomas placed it on a level with the other sacraments and maintained that it sanctified the partners for their life together.[10]

Even after Trent had defined that marriage was a true sacrament the theology of marriage lagged behind. The reason for this may have been that in Christian marriage there is no ritual sacramental sign, nothing which can be identified as matter and form. The sacramental sign is simply the exchange of consent by which husband and wife commit themselves to the marriage state. Between Christians the act of consent is the sacrament and they themselves are the ministers.

The encyclical *Casti Connubii* was a real milestone in the development of the theology of the sacrament. It indicated in detail the graces of the sacrament. In addition to the gift of sanctifying grace or the permanent principle of spiritual life, and the promise of actual grace needed for the realization of the responsibilities of marriage, it spoke of the special gifts, good impulses, and inspirations which amplify and perfect the resources of nature and which enable the partners to appreciate, accept with full decision and put into effect all that belongs to the state of wedlock with its purposes and duties.[11] Even more significantly the encyclical saw marriage as a permanent sacrament somewhat like those sacraments

---

[10]P. Adnès, *Le mariage* (Le Mystère Chrétien), Tournai 1961, pp. 89-93.
[11]n. 40.

which confer a character.[12] This concept of permanence
means more than that the efficacy of the original consent
continued throughout marriage; it also means that the
Christian marriage state is a consecrated relationship and a
permanent sign of grace. The family unit lives in an atmosphere of grace, not in virtue of any element added from outside
but from its very situation in the body of Christ. In theological terms the exchange of consent is a sacramental sign
(*sacramentum tantum*), that produces a permanent sacramental state (*res et sacramentum*) which is a constant title to
grace.

If we compare the human and Christian institutions we
shall find that every element of marriage in the order of
creation is consecrated and receives a new depth in force and
meaning in the order of the redemption.

The exchange of consent at a human level is the act in
which each accepts the other as partner for life and gives
himself to that other irrevocably so that they become one.
It is also the act by which both accept the God-given
pattern of marriage as something which pre-dates and
specifies their consent. At the Christian level the consent is
the consecration to a mission, the dedication of man and
wife to the task of continuing the redemption of Christ
through their life together. They are charged with the duty
to perfect one another and to form new Christians. Given this
perspective the consent well merits its name of marriage
vows.

Love in Christian marriage becomes charity. It is no longer
just the love of man and woman; it is the love of two
Christians for one another. It is a mediation of that love
which unites the persons in the Trinity. 'God is love; he
who abides in love abides in God and God abides in him'
(1 *John* 4:16). Man and woman made in God's image
likewise love in God's image. The capacity to make this
totally free and generous self gift to another is the highest

---

[12]n. 116.

activity of the person and that which likens him most to God. Their love is also modelled on the love between Christ and the Church. 'Husbands love your wives as Christ loves the Church.'[13]

This love of Christ is total, in that he gave his life for his bride, the Church; it is permanent, in that nothing can separate the Church from the love of Christ.

The husband-wife partnership in Christian marriage is the relationship of two Christians, each assisting the other not only to earthly fulfilment but to eternal salvation. 'The unbelieving husband is consecrated through his wife, and the unbelieving wife is consecrated through her husband.'[14]

Parenthood in Christian marriage associates husband and wife with the Creator in forming new human beings, citizens of this world; it associates them with the Redeemer in forming new Christians to whom they give the life of faith. 'These little ones, eagerly and gratefully received from the hand of God, will be considered by both father and mother as a talent entrusted to them not merely to be used for their own advantage or for that of any earthly kingdom, but to be given back to God in the day of reckoning.'[15] 'It will be your duty and privilege to bring them up as good citizens of this world and worthy members of the mystical body of Christ, so that they may one day inherit his kingdom in heaven.'[16]

This combination of a secular and a sacred mission gives to Christian marriage its particular character. As a human reality it has a secular aim, to propagate the human race and to civilize the earth by diffusing love and concern for personal values. As a Christian reality it has an ecclesial aim, to be a redeeming force, a cell in the Mystical Body radiating the power of Christ in ever-widening circles, so that the Christian family becomes the leaven of the community.

---

[13]*Eph.* 5:25.
[14]1 *Cor.* 7:14.
[15]*Casti Connubii*, n. 15.
[16]From the Marriage Service in the *Roman Ritual*.

Marriage is, therefore, a Christian vocation, a consecration to a particular mission in the Church. This gives to it its own special spirituality. It is commonplace to say that Christ's invitation to sanctity is extended to everyone and that the response of the individual is conditioned by his personality and by his state in life. There is a spirituality of the priest, of the nun, of the single person, and of the married pair. Marriage is a particular form of the Christian life and provides its unique opportunities for answering Christ's invitation, 'Come follow me: be you perfect as your Father in heaven is perfect'. The Christian works out his salvation in and through marriage, not in spite of it, nor by opting out of it. This can hardly be too much emphasized. Even though the nuptial form of blessing directs the wife to imitate the holy women Rachel, Rebecca, Sara, it is strange that the liturgy does not have a term for the saintly married woman. She is described in the Common of Saints as 'neither virgin nor martyr'. Perhaps it should be recalled, too, that the sanctity of Mary was not just that of virgin but that of wife and mother.

CELIBACY

For many centuries now the Latin Church has required celibacy of those in major orders. This means in general that subdeacon, deacon or priest may not marry after ordination, and that a married man must separate from his wife before being admitted to sacred orders. By exception married men have sometimes been admitted to the Latin ministry while continuing to live with their wives. The Church has also on occasion dispensed the diriment impediment of sacred orders to allow a subdeacon, deacon, or even a priest, to contract a marriage or to validate an illicit one. But in these cases the person in question is always laicized or removed from the ministry.

The practice in the Eastern Church is not so uniform. Monks have a celibate vocation, and bishops, who are usually taken from among the monks, must be unmarried. Some rites of the Uniate Church, for example the Syro-Malabar, follow a tradition identical to that of the Latins on the question of priestly celibacy. On the other hand, the Melkites, Maronites, Ruthenians, and Armenians, may marry before ordination; they may not marry afterwards. If a priest's wife dies, remarriage may be permitted, but in that case he must resign his office and may take up some lower function or be placed in the chancellery.

The eastern tradition goes back substantially to the Code of Justinian and to the Synod of Trullo (A.D. 692). This Synod decreed that a bishop was to observe complete continence and, if he were married before consecration, his wife had to be relegated to a remote monastery. Priests, deacons and subdeacons were permitted to marry before ordination. They were strictly prohibited from marrying afterwards, even though their first wife should have died; if they did so, they were degraded. It was also decreed that if anyone should attempt to deprive a married priest, deacon, or subdeacon of his marriage rights, or if any of them should abandon his wife on the pretext of piety, he was to be deposed.

Priestly celibacy was one of the questions which came up for discussion at Vatican II. During the fourth session the Melkite Patriarch, Maximus IV Sayegh, made a strong plea in favour of the more flexible eastern tradition. He reminded the Fathers that neither Scripture nor tradition regarded celibacy as an indispensable condition for the priesthood, and that when at the Council of Nicea some Latin Fathers attempted to have a universal law of clerical celibacy enacted, the monk Paphnutius, himself a celibate, defended the traditional institution of a married priesthood, and moved the Council to accept his views. The Patriarch told the Fathers that in the Oriental Church to-day both categories of priests exist side by side, and this practice meets the case of those who wish to serve the Church but do not want to forgo marriage. 'Celibacy is the specific vocation of the monk, it is not necessarily the specific vocation of the priest as minister of the Church. Priesthood is more a function than

a state of life . . . Celibacy therefore can disappear, if it is
to the advantage of ecclesiastical office . . . In case of necessity
the priesthood must not be sacrificed to celibacy, but celibacy
to the priesthood.'[17]

The Council Fathers did accept the principle of a married
diaconate, that is of ordaining as deacons men who had
already married, but it confirmed the Latin tradition in the
matter of priestly celibacy.

> It is not, indeed, demanded by the very nature of the
> priesthood, as is evident from the practice of the primitive
> Church and from the tradition of the eastern Churches.
> In these Churches, in addition to all bishops and those
> others who by gift of grace choose to observe celibacy,
> there also exist married priests of outstanding merit.
> While this most sacred synod recommends ecclesiastical
> celibacy, it in no way intends to change that different
> discipline which lawfully prevails in eastern Churches.[18]

The New Testament witnesses to the fact that in apostolic
times celibacy was not required of priests or bishops. Peter
was a married man, and so were many of the Twelve. St Paul
reminds the Corinthians that in remaining celibate he and
Barnabas were doing something which was not strictly
obligatory for an apostle: 'Do we not have the right to be
accompanied by a wife, as the other apostles and the brothers
of the Lord and Cephas?'[19] In his directives to Timothy
and Titus Paul instructs them to choose as bishops blameless
men, husbands each of one wife.[20] This apostolic tradition
of a married clergy lends point to the question: what is the
theological justification for linking celibacy so closely with
the priesthood, and for making it a general law in the Latin
Church? The task of identifying the religious motives behind
the rule of celibacy is complicated by the fact that they have

---

[17]*The Tablet*, 11 November 1967, 1190.
[18]Decree *On the Ministry and the Life of Priests*, n. 16.
[19]1 *Cor.* 9:5.
[20]1 *Tim.* 3:2; *Titus* 1:5-8.

evolved with changing attitudes. The motives to which we appeal to-day are not those of earlier centuries.

Theology of Celibacy

Religious continence is not an original or strictly Christian phenomenon. It was already an integral part of man's religious attitude in pre-Christian times and, naturally, early Christian attitudes were coloured by this background. Researches into the Graeco-Roman concept of religious continence have shown that it was inspired by mystical and cultic motives. The mystical motive suggested that intimacy with the Divinity would be prejudiced or degraded by close relations with any human person, whereas the cultic motive emphasized that because of his sacred function the priest is called on to avoid every taint of ritual impurity.[21]

On the mystical side the solitary life which characterized many ascetics in the Graeco-Roman and Judean world found a ready answer in the early Christian monastic movement with its sense of being alone with God. The attitudes of withdrawal from the world professed by the Christian hermits in the Thebaid were powerful motives for celibacy. Anyone who reads the literature on *de fuga mundi* or *de laudibus eremi* sees immediately that it was written by celibates for celibates. This ideal has preserved its force right down to the present day in the eastern monastic tradition.

For *priestly* celibacy the reason which carried real conviction was that of ritual purity: sex was a carnal experience which defiled a person and made him unclean and unfit for Church service. The idea that sex was unclean, that it subjected one to malign influence can be documented right across the spectrum of religious history from Greece to Rome and from India to Mexico. The Roman Vestal Virgins and the celibate priests of the Syrian *Magna Mater* have many

---

[21]This background has been examined by E. Fehrle, *Die kultische Keuscheit im Altertum*, Giessen 1919, and H. Jeanmaire, 'Sexualité et mysticisme dans les anciennes sociétés helléniques' in *Mystique et Continence* (Etudes Carmélitaines), Paris-Bruges 1952.

N

parallels. The Old Testament is no exception. When Moses sanctified the people for the theophany on Mount Sinai he directed them to 'have no intercourse with any woman'.[22] In its long list of legal impurities on matters of sex the Book of Leviticus includes marital intercourse: 'If a man lies carnally with a woman they shall both bathe in water and be unclean until evening.'[23] Ahimelech the priest agreed to give the holy bread of proposition to the starving David and his men 'if they be clean especially from women'.[24]

This attitude found a ready response in the early Church. It gained particular force from the tendency to identify sexual passion with the carnal concupiscence which was seen as the peculiar effect of the Fall. The St Jerome who had paraphrased St Paul's statement that 'It is well for a man not to touch a woman'[25] as 'It is bad for a man to touch a woman' had no scruples in making the unqualified statement *omnis coitus immundus*. This was a conviction which died very hard; traces of it survived to our own day in the terminology which called marriage chastity imperfect, and in the spirituality which required sexual abstinence as a preparation for the reception of the Eucharist: 'Whoever comes to receive the Sacrament at Mass after being contaminated by the sex act dishonours and desecrates the divine service.'[26] These words of Origen express an attitude which survived down the ages through Sanchez and St Alphonsus to our own day when Pius X in his decree on frequent Communion effectively put an end to it.

It goes without saying that this duty of continence bound the sacrificing priest. Popes Damasus I, Siricius I, and Innocent I used almost identical terms in urging the priest to be continent and to be free from every carnal desire so that his sacrifice should be agreeable in God's sight. Damasus

[22]*Exod.* 19:15.
[23]15:18.
[24]1 *Sam.* 21:4-5.
[25]1 *Cor.* 7:1.
[26]Origen, *Hom. in Levit.* PG 12:474.

reminds priests that even their pagan counterparts practise continence in order to offer their idolatrous sacrifices. 'If intercourse is defilement the priest should be properly prepared to undertake his heavenly office. Otherwise, he who is making propitiation for the sins of others may be found unworthy himself.'[27] In later years the words of Gregory I in the ordination formula *Imitamini quod tractatis* were interpreted along these same lines – the priest who celebrates the death of Christ is called on to preserve his body from every carnal act or desire. The popular preacher began where the theologian left off, and omitted many qualifications in order to get more punch into his words. Peter Damian's *De Caelibatu Sacerdotum* is a good example of this. The strength and universality of this tradition is evident from the fact that the Eastern Church enjoined continence on its married clergy for a day or days before they celebrated the Eucharist. This was an explicit requirement in the Trullan Synod of 692.

As one traces the path of these motives down the centuries one notes that the chief emphasis was on the concept of purity from carnal indulgence, something which required not only celibacy but continence. This was virginal purity in the case of monks and ritual purity in the case of the priests.

Under the influence of the theologians and canonists of the twelfth century the idea of ordination as a commitment to a way of life comes to the fore. The priest comes to be seen as more than a functionary fulfilling a sacred ministry. He is a man totally committed to following Christ. Celibacy is required of him not just as cultic purity but as part of the way of life of one who has left all things for the sake of the kingdom of Heaven. Detachment is the key word here; the priest who is a true follower of Christ is singled out by the virtues which express detachment, for example humility, poverty and celibacy. The canonists can claim a good deal of credit for the development of these views, which are the

---

[27]*Synodal Letter*, PL 13:1186.

beginning of a real spirituality of the priesthood. One of their major contributions was the teaching that the obligation of celibacy arose not because general law imposed it but because the individual pledged himself by vow to observe it. In this way the celibacy of the priest was presented as a charism, as free an undertaking as that of the monk. Celibacy was not just a condition imposed on the priest from without; it was an integral part of the way of life which he undertook, and it underlined the supernatural values for which he stood.

The theological ideals which we have singled out are only part of a whole context of motivation – a lot of which was aimed at showing that celibacy was the only practicable state for the priest, that celibacy placed him more completely at the disposal of his bishop in the matter of ecclesiastical appointments, that it safeguarded Church property and saved the Church the expense of supporting a married clergy, that the knowledge that a priest was continent made his preaching on continence more credible to his flock.

What distinguishes the contemporary theology of celibacy from older teaching and attitudes is that it finds inspiration directly in the New Testament teaching on the nature of the apostolate. This enables it to short-circuit misunderstandings occasioned by the traditional motives of mystical intimacy or ritual purity. Firstly, the love which the God of Christianity demands is not isolated in a vacuum or in a solitude outside life; far from excluding human love or contact with one's neighbour it is expressed and proved in and through this love and contact. Secondly it is difficult to claim that the marriage act implies ritual uncleanness when the Vatican Council tells us: 'The acts themselves which are proper to conjugal love and which are exercised in accord with genuine human dignity must be honoured with great reverence.'[28]

The theology of celibacy which one finds in the Council documents and in Pope Paul's encyclical on celibacy is

---

[28]Constitution *On the Church in the Modern World*, n. 51.

centred on the person of Christ and on the nature of his life work. Celibacy is proposed as *apostolic* (it serves the kingdom), *eschatological* (it is a sign of the kingdom), and *Christological* (it identifies the priest with the Redeemer). 'Through virginity or celibacy observed for the kingdom of heaven priests are consecrated to Christ by a new and exceptional reason. They adhere to him more easily with an undivided heart, they dedicate themselves more freely in him and through him to the service of God and men, and they more expeditiously minister to his kingdom and the work of heavenly regeneration . . . They give, moreover, a living sign of the world to come, by faith and charity already made present.'[29]

That these three elements must be the central ones in a theology of celibacy is suggested by Christ's words in the Gospels. In Matthew 19:12 he speaks of those chosen ones who have renounced marriage for the sake of the kingdom: 'There are eunuchs who have made themselves eunuchs for the sake of the kingdom of heaven.' In Mark 10:29 he reassures his followers who have left house and family 'for my sake and for the Gospel' that they have not chosen in vain. In Luke 14:26–27 he says: 'If somebody comes to me and does not hate his father and mother and wife and children and brothers and sisters and even his own soul, he cannot be my disciple.' In these texts the phrases 'for my sake' and 'for the sake of the kingdom of heaven' do not just mean 'in order to achieve salvation'. They mean 'to share my work of preaching the kingdom', with all that this implies.

Celibacy is called *apostolic* because its purpose is to place a particular Christian free from all family and secular concerns wholly at the service of Christ and of the Church. It is motivated by the apostle's love for the Master, leaving all things that he may follow him with complete self-dedication. This apostolic ideal of total detachment is glossed by St Paul in 1 Corinthians 7:32–34: 'The unmarried man is anxious

---

[29]Decree *On the Ministry and Life of Priests*, n. 16.

about the affairs of the Lord, how to please the Lord. But the married man is anxious about worldly affairs, how to please his wife, and his interests are divided.'

The consecration to Christ, by virtue of a new and lofty title like celibacy evidently gives to the priest, even in the practical field, the maximum efficiency and the best disposition of mind, psychologically and affectively, for the continuous exercise of a perfect charity. This charity will permit him to spend himself wholly for the welfare of all, in a fuller and more concrete way. It also guarantees him obviously a greater freedom and flexibility in the pastoral ministry, it is active and loving presence in the world, to which Christ has invited him, so that he may pay fully to all the children of God the debt due to them.[30]

Celibacy as *eschatological* is the aspect which comes in for particular emphasis in contemporary theology. In effect it is nothing more than a specific application of the apostolic dimension. It makes celibacy a prophecy in act, a sign to the world which proclaims that the kingdom of God is the one thing really necessary and that it takes precedence over all temporal concerns. The Kingdom is an eschatological reality. It is over and above time. It is at once of the present and of the future. Christian celibacy proclaims the transience of the world and it anticipates the final transformation. In it world patterns are set aside in favour of the life of the spirit. It announces clearer than any spoken word 'our common wealth is in heaven'. It is then a sign of Christian hope. Marriage implies an attachment to human persons and the acceptance of earthly values; celibacy as a specifically Christian sign implies an attachment to the heavenly Christ.

In the world of man, so deeply involved in earthly concerns and too often enslaved by the desires of the flesh, the

---

[30]Paul VI, *On Priestly Celibacy*, n. 32.

precious divine gift of perfect continence for the kingdom of heaven stands out precisely as a singular sign of the blessings of heaven, it proclaims the presence on earth of the final stages of salvation with the arrival of a new world, and in a way it anticipates the fulfilment of the kingdom as it sets forth the supreme values which will one day shine forth in all the children of God. This continence, therefore, stands as a testimony to the necessary progress of the People of God towards the final goal of their earthly pilgrimage, and as a stimulus for all to raise their eyes to the things above, where Christ sits at the right hand of the Father and where our life is hidden in Christ with God until he appears in glory.[31]

Celibacy is *Christological* because it identifies the priest in a particular way with Christ and with his mission. It is not just a question of imitating Christ's personal celibacy. Christ was celibate not because he avoided marriage but because he was completely dedicated to the mission of saving all men, a task which demanded freedom from family responsibilities. 'Who is my mother and who are my brothers? And stretching out his hand towards his disciples he said: "Here are my mother and my brothers. For whoever does the will of my Father in heaven he is my brother and sister and mother." '[32] His disciples are called to have the same detachment in carrying out their mission in association with him: 'He who loves father or mother more than me is not worthy of me; and he who loves son or daughter more than me is not worthy of me.'[33] Christ's life is a concrete example of the apostolic and eschatological, and it is here that priests are called to imitate him.

Christ, the only Son of the Father, by the power of the Incarnation itself was made mediator between heaven and earth, between the Father and the human race.

---

[31]*Ibid.*, n. 34.
[32]*Matt.* 12:48-50.
[33]*Matt.* 10:37.

Wholly in accord with this mission, Christ remained throughout his whole life in the state of celibacy, which signified his total dedication to the service of God and men. This deep connection between celibacy and the priesthood of Christ is reflected in those whose fortune it is to share in the dignity and in the mission of the mediator and eternal Priest; this sharing will be more perfect the freer the sacred minister is from the bonds of flesh and blood.[34]

The words *'freedom from* the bonds of flesh and blood' mean *free for* the following of Christ and all that this implies. The following of Christ is not a shirking of responsibility but an acceptance of responsibility; it is not flight but a full commitment to everything that being a man and being a Christian implies; it is not a rejection of love or a limitation of one's power to love but a readiness to respond in love and to extend this response until, if possible, it is as total and as all-embracing as the love of Christ.

St Paul's direction 'Let that mind be in you which was in Christ Jesus'[35] applies in a particular way to those who follow Christ as the ministers and preachers of his kingdom. By *mind* we mean his attitudes not only to his specific mission of redemption but to all that being a man among men implies. We find, for example, that his celibacy did not cut him off from sympathy with his fellows or from human friendship. In his account of the raising of Lazarus from the dead St John tells us of the very close friendship which bound Christ to the family of Bethany: 'Jesus loved Martha and her sister and Lazarus.'[36]

CONCLUSION

In the above pages we have dealt separately with marriage and celibacy as two states of Christian life. It may be invidious to compare the two but Christian teaching forces

[34]Paul VI, *loc. cit.* n. 21.
[35]*Phil.* 2:5.
[36]*John* 11:5.

this comparison. The debate which the comparison implies
is nothing new. It is already a live question in the Pauline
epistles and is a familiar theme in patristic literature. The
Council of Trent solemnly defined what the Christian
decision must be on the relative merits of these alternatives:
'If anyone shall say that the married state is to be preferred
to the state of virginity or celibacy, and that it is not more
excellent and blessed to remain in the state of virginity or
celibacy than to be joined in marriage, let him be
anathema.'[37]

A number of important qualifications are implied in this
statement. The contrast, marriage versus celibacy, does not
suggest a straight contest between good and evil. It is a
question of comparative judgement, of a choice between two
alternative Christian goods. Indeed, the better one's understanding of marriage and the more wholesome one's attitude
to sex, the greater one's appreciation of celibacy will be. It
is not defined that celibacy is a way of greater holiness for
any particular individual. St Paul said: 'I wish that all were
as I myself am; but each has his own special gift from God, one
of one kind and one of another.'[38] Neither does the definition
attach any excellence to the material fact of remaining single.
Non-marriage is an ambiguous and neutral reality, and,
after all, bachelorhood may be nothing more than the selfish
avoidance of responsibility. What is defined is that virginity
as a Christian institution, with the motives and qualities
traditionally implied in this description, is a higher state
than that of marriage, even Christian marriage. Again
St Paul tells us that while there are many charisms and
vocations in the Church, some are superior to others:
'Earnestly desire the higher gifts.'[39]

It is hardly necessary to remark that the actual experience
of marriage or celibacy only approximates to the ideal. The
aspirant to either side brings with him his individual defects

---

[37]*Denz.* n. 980.
[38]1 *Cor.* 7:7.
[39]1 *Cor.* 12:31.

of character, which the chosen state will not remedy; both states also embody responsibilities which may become personal problems. The individual himself may have a blind spot which gives him quite an unbalanced view of his duties of state. The father of a family may be faithful to his wife and support his children financially, and then feel quite justified in his belief that he is an exemplary husband and parent, even though his wife does not experience any real companionship from him and even though he is harsh and careless in the home. The mere fact that a priest is celibate is no guarantee that his life is apostolic or that it is a sign of the kingdom; in fact everything which his life actually is may belie the promise of his celibacy. This will occur more easily where celibacy and other aspects of the priesthood are seen as mere legal impositions rather than as a way of life to which one has generously pledged oneself. If a priest sees celibacy in terms of law, the values which his celibacy should represent may be more than neutralized by types of egocentricity and worldiness with which the law does not explicitly deal – selfishness, hypochondria, expensive and time-consuming hobbies, avarice. These are the stock compensations of the celibate.

The Last Things:
God Reveals his Glory

Donal Flanagan

The end of our lives, if we are to believe our own spiritual literature, is something we shy away from in fear and terror because it is a facing up to a stern Judge. Donal Davoren, the agnostic hero of *The Shadow of a Gunman,* taunts the terrified Christian, Seamus Shields during the Black and Tan raid: 'I leave the fear of death to the people who are always praying for eternal life'. If the remark annoys us is it perhaps because O'Casey has struck closer to the truth than we find it comfortable to admit?

If we envisage hell and heaven somehow as a fifty-fifty chance shouldn't we ask ourselves what meaning do we give to 'the good news of salvation'? Is God who so loved the world that he gave his only-begotten Son that we should not perish, uncertain in his purpose or lacking power? What do we mean by living in the certainty of Christian hope?

Our approach to the Last Things is individualistic, fear-filled, and spiritualistic. We tend all the time to talk about the salvation of *the soul.* Salvation appears as spiritual salvation, not bodily salvation. But we are a body as well as a soul, even if we normally say – and this is revealing – that we have a body. If we look at the manuals of eschatology, (that section of theology which deals with the last things) we find that the treatment of the Last Things is marked by these

three same characteristics that we have already mentioned·
The manuals of eschatology deal first and at length with
death, judgement, hell and heaven, with what they term
individual eschatology. They concentrate on salvation as
salvation of the soul. Then later on in the tract and almost
by way of appendix, they deal with collective eschatology,
and with the integral nature of salvation, i.e. the resurrection
of the flesh and the final consummation.

When we turn from the perspectives of the manuals and of
our popular eschatology to the Scriptures we notice a
difference. We find in fact that the scriptural presentation
of the last things is first of all more collective than individualistic in its emphasis It is, secondly, integral as opposed to
what we have called over-spiritual. Scripture presents completed salvation as a total salvation of man as he is. Thirdly,
the note which pervades the eschatological statements of
Scripture – those statements of Scripture which deal with
the end of time – is not the note of fear of judgement, though
this is preached, it is rather the note of expectant joy. The
typical scriptural word to describe this emphasis is the word
Maran-atha which means 'Come Lord'.

We offer here an analysis of some of the qualities of final
salvation which are indicated in the Scriptures. Firstly, all
through Scripture the last things are seen as in continuity with
our present Christian existence. They are, in fact, already
present in our Christian lives in a hidden way. The kingdom
is not something far off in the future, it is being realized
hiddenly here and now. Or to say this in another way, we
have now not merely the promise of the Spirit, we have *the
Spirit already given to us* in our ordinary daily humdrum
earthly lives. The Spirit works now binding men to one
another in Christ. The first epistle of St John brings out this
present and hidden glory very clearly: 'See what love the
Father has given us that we should be called the children of
God. And so we are. The reason why the world does not
know us is that it did not know him. Beloved, we are God's
children even now and it does not yet appear what we shall

be, but we know that when he appears we shall be like him,
for we shall see him as he is' (*John* 3:1, 2). This continuity
of the end salvation with the salvation already given is underlined in the constant call of the New Testament writers for
endurance. For the New Testament writers, the Christian
is already in Christ. He must suffer and endure a little while
and then his present glorious state will be revealed in its
fulness. This is made plain in the first epistle of St Peter:
'Blessed be the God and the Father of our Lord Jesus Christ,
by his mercy we have been born anew to a living hope,
through the resurrection of Jesus Christ from the dead, and
through an inheritance which is imperishable, undefiled,
unfading, kept in heaven for you. You who by God's power
are guarded through faith for a salvation which is ready *to be
revealed* in the last times. In this you rejoice though now for
a little while you may have to suffer various trials' (1 *Pet.*
1:3–6).

A second quality of final salvation which emerges from the
scriptural accounts is its otherness. Although continuous
with our present Christian existence it is a life which is not
the same as the life we live now. And yet it is not entirely
different. It is a human life, but a human life lived in another
mode. While Scripture is very clear on the fact of this other
existence it is by no means so clear on the nature of it, and
this is something which we have to face. We see this problem
in the obscurity of the long text in the first epistle to the
Corinthians, chapter 15, which St Paul dedicates to the
nature of the risen life. Paul poses the question about the
nature of this life. How are the dead raised, what kind of
bodies do they have? And when you analyse Paul's answer
to this question you find that he says surprisingly little. He
says, in fact, simply that the life which those raised with
Christ will know, is a life of a different kind than we know
here (1 *Cor.* 15:35–57.)

This does, however, give us a general principle from
which we can conclude many things, for Scripture reveals
to us that Christ's salvation is an *integral* salvation,

that is to say it encompasses the whole man as an embodied spirit. Salvation reaches man in the concrete fleshly existence which he has in this world. It takes account of man's existence as a social being and saves him as such a being. Scripture again makes clear that salvation reaches man as existing within a material universe to which he is the key, and which finds expression in and through him. Man is saved, then, not from these things, but in them and with them. He is not saved as a soul because he is not just a soul; he is not saved alone because he is not alone; he is not saved as detached from the material universe because he belongs in and with the material universe. He is not saved from those qualifications of his human existence which we designate as community and universe, he is saved with them and they are saved with him.

Paul must be taken seriously then when he talks about the creation 'groaning in travail'. The full text reads, 'I consider that the sufferings of this present time are not worthy to be compared with the glory which is to be revealed in us, for the creation waits with eager longing for the revealing of the sons of God. Creation was subjected to futility, not of its own will but by the will of him who subjected it in hope, because creation itself will be set free from its bondage to decay and attain the glorious liberty of the children of God. We know that the whole creation has been groaning in pain together until now, and not only the creation, but we ourselves who have the first fruits of the Spirit and groan inwardly as we wait our adoption as sons, the redemption of our bodies' (*Rom.* 8:18-23).

Completed salvation then, according to Scripture, is an integral salvation. Scripture teaches us to look forward to a fully human salvation, a salvation which takes account of the bodily and social aspects of man and which has even a cosmic dimension.

I should like now to consider one of the great eschatological themes of the New Testament, the Parousia or the coming of Christ, according to the synoptic Gospels (see

Mark 13:24 f. Cf. *Matt.* 24:15 f.) the coming of the Son of
Man in the glory of the Father, with the angels, a coming
on the clouds with power and glory. This coming will be
preceded by signs in the heavens, by the departure of the
heavenly bodies from their courses. It will be like a flash
of lightning – Christ will come, we are told in the Acts of
the Apostles, 'as he ascended into heaven', and he will
take, on his coming, his throne in the heavens. The time,
however, of this event, as far as we can make out from
scriptural evidence, is indefinite. This is underlined in many
of the parables which preach readiness for the coming of the
Son of Man (see *Matt.* 25:1-13).

The imagery in which the New Testament portrays the
Second Coming, the Parousia, is derived from the book of
Daniel, especially the seventh chapter where the coming of
one 'like a Son of Man' is described. In Daniel, this coming
is the last act of world history. It represents the definitive
establishment of God's reign and rule over the world and the
subjection of all powers hostile to God. Early Christian
tradition seems to have been inspired by the words of Our
Lord to apply this apocalyptic imagery to Jesus himself.
St Paul in his writings presents the Parousia in much the
same way as the Synoptics, referring to it as *the day of Our
Lord Jesus Christ*.

The imagery in which the Parousia is presented in
Scripture has made its way into much Christian art, and
indeed into much Christian preaching. We must never
forget that this imagery stems from a tradition of apocalyptic
writing and must be interpreted and understood within this
tradition. We are not then to take it as if it were a press
release of our own day detailing the programme of a future
state visit. This highly symbolic literary form cannot be
handled as if it were a newspaper report. Thus it would seem
hazardous to draw from this imagery any conclusions about
the external features of the Parousia. The basic fact of faith
that there will be a term to history which God himself sets,
that there will be a definitive vindication of God and a

definitive and final overwhelming of evil – this much is clear and pertains to the substance of the faith, but the imagery, in which these truths come to us, does not. Scripture gives us no warrant for insisting on the details of the manner of Christ's coming.

The early Church looked forward in hope and expectation to the Parousia. The Christians saw the coming of Jesus, this time not in humiliation, but in glory, as the consummation of his work and of history and of God's providence for the world. They felt that as God had realized in Jesus himself the glory of the last times immediately after his humiliation in death, so he would in the return of Jesus realize quickly the glory of the last times in those who had died with Jesus in baptism and were awaiting his glory. This expectation of the revelation of Christ's glory, as St Peter calls it in the first chapter of his first epistle, this eager looking forward to the consummation of the world and of all things in Christ's reappearance, is a constant and most touching feature of the New Testament writings. Paul, at the end of his long letter to the Corinthians in which he has busied himself with dogmatic and pastoral questions which are causing him concern, with the day-to-day in-the-world problems of his Church, closes his final greeting with the word *Maran-atha*, (Lord, come). This word indicates clearly that neither he nor his fellow Christians, even when immersed in the tasks of evangelization, of establishing the Church in every place, ever lost sight of the pilgrim nature of this Church. They lived not in a state of fear but in one of lively expectation of the second coming of Jesus. This was not something to be feared but something to be longed for, something to be keenly desired. This particular term, *Maran-atha*, is Aramaic and seems to go back to the very earliest Christian community of Jerusalem. Its preservation in Paul, in Aramaic, untranslated, is an indication of the venerable character it had already at the time that Paul was writing. It is clear evidence of the eschatological orientation of the faith of this early Christian community. There is then in Paul, an emphasis on the glory which is awaited, the glory of the expected end. He writes: 'When Christ who is our life appears, then you also will appear with him in glory' (*Col.* 3:4).

In the Apocalypse, the last and most obscure of the books of the New Testament, we find again the same looking forward to Jesus's coming with love and eagerness. Christ says, to the Church of Philadephia which is undergoing persecution: 'I am coming soon, hold fast', (*Apoc.* 3:11) and these words of consolation directed to the persecuted Church, envisage Christ's coming as deliverance, as victory, as glory. The Apocalypse itself closes with the words of the triumphant Jesus, 'Surely I am coming soon' and to this the writer of the Apocalypse responds in the prayer, "Come Lord Jesus" (*Apoc.* 22:20). The pilgrim Church repeats this plea for the glory of her Lord Jesus to be revealed speedily. The Church calls to the Lord in the Spirit who dwells in her. 'And the Spirit and the Bride say "Come" ' (*Apoc.* 22:17).

The Parousia so eagerly awaited by the first Christians will reveal the consummation of history, of the history of Christ and of the history of the world, in God who will be directly revealed in his glory. The glorification of Christ begun already in his resurrection is part of a single process which continues in the saving history of every man and of the whole community of salvation, drawing the world into God's transfiguring self-communication. Man can refuse to accept this communication for himself. Man can even finally reject God's gift of himself and in this rejection pronounce his own judgement, but he cannot hinder this divine development. The completion of this transfiguring process whose length is hidden from us, is Christ's Parousia. The risen Lord will then be revealed to all as the beginning of the End, as the source of this process, as its central meaning and its climax. The Parousia reveals the Whole Christ.

o

Hope:
Going Forward to Christ

ENDA McDONAGH

God's self-giving to man and man's response to God achieved its definitive stage in Christ. In him the reign of God in the world was established. Yet that reign has not attained its final completion. There is a tension in us and in our world between what is and what is to be. The self gift of God as our salvation is also our task. We have to become what we, by the grace of God, are. We are saved but as yet in hope.

This tension between what is and what is yet to be in the individual man, in the human community and in the world or cosmos taken as a whole, provides the driving force and the sense of direction for human moral activity. The human moral task is, in the light of revelation in Christ, the working out of that kingdom which is within us, which has been achieved for all in the risen Christ. In him mankind, individually and as a community, and the created physical world to which man belongs, have broken through to the destiny to which they have been called, the fulfilment and transformation which immediate presence to the Father involves. The first-born of all creation shares his transformation with us as we shared our human and cosmic natures with him. This share which has been given us must grow to the fulness of his. In the implementing of this task, man is borne on the assurance of Christ's achievement and promise.

He is carried forward by hope to seek his destiny in and through his life here on earth, in and through his moral activity.

The force of the eschatological dimension of the Christian message is to reveal to man the journey which lies before him and at the same time to give him the courage and energy to undertake that journey into the unknown. The hope that is born of Christ is essential to all Christian living and activity.

Moral activity then is about achieving the maturity to which all men and indeed the cosmos are called. To discuss this further it will be useful to take in turn the call to maturity as it applies to each of the three elements in creation to which Christian eschatology refers, the individual human being, the human community and the cosmos in general. In this way the doctrinal teaching outlined in the previous lecture will find in its extension to Christian living its moral application.

Here it is necessary to mention one obvious misinterpretation which any approach to morality based on future fulfilment does not easily avoid. And it is a misinterpretation which has always played a part in popular teaching about the Christian way of life. 'Pie in the sky or at least at the end of the road' would be a fair if crude description of this understanding of the shape of Christian living. The end of the road and the pie are reached by following the directions given but they simply point the way along a road that has nothing to offer itself. The journey in itself is meaningless and should be got through as quickly and as painlessly as possible. Such an attitude implies contempt for, or at least indifference to, the world as a road through which one has to travel and has led some within and without the Christian Church to believe that Christianity is in principle opposed to the human and the cosmic.

The fact of the incarnation ought to be sufficient disproof of this, but the becoming man and cosmic of the second Person in the triune God has not always been so clearly

P

understood. Exclusive attention to Christ's divinity to the neglect of his humanity combined with an escapist notion of life beyond this world do mislead many Christians about the nature of Christian life. The future kingdom and the hope of it to be discussed here are already in action in this life and in this world. The future is the fuller realization of the present. There is no way to that future fulfilment except through the present. There is no escaping this world into some celestial haven. It is not possible to sit down and await the second coming of Christ. What is at stake might well be better described as our arrival at the stage at which he is. And while the arrival is his gift to us, it is not achieved by following blindly any rules of the road or by ignoring the road itself. It is in and through the present moment that the future is realized. Nobody should take the present in all its dimensions more seriously than the Christian for whom it is laden with the eternal and the divine.

The tension between what is and what is to be gives the Christian a morality orientated towards the future but not one that allows him to evade the present. The polarizing force exercised by *ta eschata*, the Last Things, is not a distraction from his task in this world but the source of its ultimate meaning and urgency. The hope that is his in Christ is for the development and transformation of the human and the cosmic after the manner of their development in the risen Christ, the completion or the final maturity of the man who was God. This maturity is offered, given and finally assured to men and the world in Christ our hope.

To draw out the implications of Christian eschatology for Christian living according to the three dimensions of man-in-the-world already listed, the individual, community and cosmic, it is more convenient for historical and theological, if not entirely logical, reasons to begin with the community dimension.

Hope and the Community

God addressed himself to mankind as a whole from the

very beginning. He spoke to man in community. The individuals to whom he spoke were always the representatives of the wider community with which he wished to initiate or develop this personal relationship. The dynamism of this relationship, the promise which it carried within itself was directed towards the establishment of a kingdom or community. The completion of God's relationship with man was always visualized in social terms.

The community dimension of Yahweh's relationship with man in the Old Testament is too obvious to be laboured here. Its relevance for this discussion is precisely in its presentation not only as given but as still to be achieved in a new and fuller way. God's dealings with his people build on his present choice and protection of them, their hope of future fulfilment. The Old Testament itself has been well described as a book of hope. Its point lies in the future beyond itself but that point is assured by promises and their guarantee in the power and fidelity of Yahweh.

The contour of hope in God's dealings with his people emerges in the call of Abraham to which the Israelites traced their choice as Yahweh's special people. It was a call into an unknown land and for the sake of posterity to a man without any children who had an aged wife. The only basis on which it could be answered was that of recognition of Yahweh in faith for what he was and the trust or hope which that inspired.

In the consciousness of Israel their proper formation as a people and as Yahweh's people was realized in the events of the Exodus and the covenant on Sinai. The Exodus itself is a typical "Hope Happening" in its leading the Israelites out of captivity into a new and promised land by the power and fidelity of Yahweh. On its basis the Mosaic Covenant is formed and the relationship between Yahweh and his people reaches a climactic stage. At Sinai the events of Exodus are cited in proof of Yahweh's giving himself to his people and the response demanded in return is given concrete shape in the Decalogue.

The Mosaic Covenant becomes in its turn the source of the further hope of Israel. The religion retains its openness to the future. There is a still greater future awaiting Yahweh's people not based indeed on their own merits but always on the loving mercy of Yahweh and his fidelity to his commitment in choosing this people. The hope of the Old Testament receives its particular poignancy and urgency from the persistent failure of the people of God's choice to respond in kind. Their sins highlight the loving mercy and fidelity of God who in the face of this human weakness appears more fully as the sole ground of their hope. It is not simply man's inability to foresee the future through which he must attain his destiny, that is, come to his God, that makes trust in God necessary for him. It is above all his sense of his own weakness based on his continued experience of his sinning.

With the achievement of the hope of the first Israel in Jesus Christ these features of a call into the unknown of God's people and their weakness in responding continue to characterize the subject of this hope, the new Israel. Of course the new Israel lives in the context of the new Covenant. The definitive stage has been reached. These are the last days. The kingdom is amongst us. Yet its complete realization lies ahead and there is no access to it except through the ambiguities of human history. The Christ who has triumphed over sin and the law and death is present to us and in us. He is present in the world in his people but that presence is still obscure because still incomplete. The becoming man and cosmic of God has a future as well as a past. The life, death and resurrection of Jesus Christ is promise as well as achievement. When all things are taken up to him, submitted to his lordship, the incarnation will be complete (1 *Cor.* 15). The people which now shows forth this incarnation in the world, bears the marks of the achieved and the yet to be. It is a pilgrim people on the way to the land which God will show it, not a people already in the triumphant security of its homeland. Where the Church gives the impression of being already in possession, of having arrived, it betrays the trust that has been given to it. The life of the Church must be understood and experienced as the wayfaring life which it really is. The Christian life in community is a venturing into the unknown, not a sheltering from dangers and darkness in some imagined fortress of the past.

Vatican II will have accomplished a great deal if it has restored the restlessness and insecurity which ought to characterize God's people here below. So far from regretting the disturbance of settled ways the Church should give thanks for the fresh awareness of its condition of pilgrimage, as going forward in the half-light of faith which the Spirit has given it. This darkness of the road is rendered more dangerous by our sinfulness so that we may wander off in wrong directions. The greater sin however is to use this fear of human weakness to opt out of the journey altogether or to pretend that we have already arrived. On the one hand we decline the call of the Father completely, on the other we substitute a destiny of our own making for his. In either case we fail to recognize the God of Abraham, of Isaac and of Jesus Christ as the God who lies ahead and who, through no merits of ours, but in fidelity to his promises, brings us to him if we will only trust him.

For clergy and laity the temptation to rest where we are, and regard any summons to go forward as a delusion, is always very strong. Today that temptation is naturally in evidence because the summons forward has sounded loud and clear. The forms of the temptation are manifold. For the bishop or priest or somebody with special responsibility in the Church this is likely to be a fear of upsetting the 'simple faithful' or a complacency about the level of outward Christianity that may be evident, or the simple fear of the unknown which may be a tribute to man's weakness but takes little account of the saving power of God. The examples usually cited of the danger of change are often capable of more than one interpretation and should always be balanced by examples of failure to change. Of course the argument

cannot be decided by appeal to any such historical evidence
when the very essence of the life of God's people consists in
following him into the unknown, in changing. Change,
development, growth, going forward in the dark and so
risking – these are of the essence of Christianity as the
embodiment of its hope. The obligation of pastors in
particular is not to eliminate the risk, still less to prevent the
growth. It is rather to stimulate the growth by taking the
risk, not on the basis of selfish human calculation but out of
loving reflection on the self-giving of God in Christ as
mediated above all in his written word and in prayerful
trust in the holy Spirit.

The laity may well be disturbed and this may be a
necessary part of the struggling forward of the Church.
Their temptation often takes the form of needing the
spiritual security of a religion which is consoling but not
challenging. It allows them to get on with their own
comfortable lives and at the same time provides escape from
the shattering effect the ultimate situations like death might
have. For too many prosperous Christians the attentions of
'Holy Mother Church' are much too soothing.

The full measure of the hopeful and venturing character of
God's people is realized only when its vocation is understood
in relation to the rest of the world. From the very beginning,
God's call of a particular people was not for its own sake,
but for the sake of all mankind. To Abraham and Isaac it
was made clear that the promise was not directed to their
posterity alone, but that in them, all the nations of the earth
would be blessed. The role of the chosen people as manifest
in their history was to bring salvation, the knowledge and
love of the one true God to all men. Although this became
increasingly clear in the prophets, it was with the coming of
Christ that the universality of the Father's offer became
fully evident. He was the new head of the race. In him, and
only in him, men had access to the Father, to their final
destiny. His presence and his way to the Father would be
realized and shown forth in the world by that body the

Church, of which he is head. By his own presence and through the gift of the Spirit, the new people of God would act as the bridge-head for mankind in its striving for its destiny. As the human race seeks its fulness or maturity, that people in which God visibly manifests his presence has the duty of acting as the *avant-garde*. The Church must be a sign of the future of mankind. It must witness to the reality of such a future by entering fully into the shaping of that future which, while it is ultimately a gift of God, it is so on the model of the incarnation, in and through the human and the cosmic.

In the present context that future is above all a community future. The call to be sons of the Father and brothers of one another is addressed to all. The final destiny is the complete realization of that sonship and brotherhood. It is the full realization of the emerging human community. As the first earnest of that completed community the Church must co-operate with every force which seeks to remove the barriers between men and to build a genuine and lasting human community. In this work the developing community will be aware that final completion lies outside history and that above all, this cannot be achieved by human means alone. Indeed it will recognize and expect the frequent failures which as a human enterprise it will suffer because of the selfishness or sin of man. This will not be the effect of its abandoning the work as humanly impossible or of leaving it in passive fashion to a God who has no need of men. It will rather stimulate to greater deeds 'in the flesh' or in human fashion, in the confidence of the redemption accomplished in the flesh by Christ.

The hope of a Christian community is a hope for the whole community of mankind. It would be a serious betrayal if it did not show that hope in deed as well as in word by its readiness to follow its Master in risking all for the sake of mankind, exposing itself to danger of hurt and failure. Not every risk is a God-seeking or neighbour-seeking one. Self-seeking may insert itself here as elsewhere. The self-seeking

which occurs may take the form of presumption, because a
man too easily presumes that he knows where God is
calling him. Some of the current difficulties within the
Church are due to this presumption. The Christian who is
aware of his vocation to move forward (and this is the
vocation of every Christian) must try to see this in the true
setting of his service to God and neighbour or community.
This does not mean that he can never risk being wrong when
it is an inescapable part of being human. If he is serious about
moving towards God he will try to reduce the risk of error
as much as possible. And it certainly does not mean that he
may never risk disturbing neighbour or community.
Disturbance may be exactly what is needed. He will try to
make this a creative rather than a destructive disturbance.
Whatever disturbance there is should be for the building up
of the body of Christ, not for its disruption. Such a creative
disturbance may also be very painful and meet with
opposition from other members of the community with and
without office, with and without the best interests of the
community at heart. It is not the task of the disturber or
disturbed to judge their opponents' sincerity, but to bear
witness to the truth in mutual love, so that they may find
the next step forward on the way to the Father to which they
are continually summoned in Jesus Christ.

To do this in a creative and constructive manner demands
both humility and confidence, confidence not in self but in
God and in his power to bring the other and oneself further
along the road in understanding and serving his truth. The
most destructive force in a Christian community, as it seeks
the maturity demanded of it, is a corroding distrust which
can separate clergy and laity, priests and bishops, theologians
and magisterium. It turns what should be creative differences
into destructive quarrels, so that the permanent growing
pains of the community and individuals become the
deliberate wounds of war between brothers. There is some
danger of that in the Church today. There is some evidence
of lack of trust in God and one another under his grace.

There is some unawareness of God's constant call to his pilgrim Church to move forward, on the one side, and some insensitivity to the difficulties of readily deciphering and responding to this call, on the other. There is some lack of genuine Christian hope.

The Hope of the Individual Person

The individual Christian life which can be lived only in community can be no less pilgrim than that of the community as a whole. And apart from the Christian's direct obligations to the hope of the community, his personal life must also bear the stamp of the Christian virtue so characteristic of our interim situation. For the individual, his personal, moral activity takes him along the road towards God, not in isolation of course, but nevertheless as a personal step which can be taken by nobody else but him. It is a step which he must also take to a certain extent in the dark. Every mortal action which is born as we have seen of faith, of his awareness of God inviting him, cannot enjoy more than the half-light which faith offers. It is not trust in his own judgement which enables him to take this step, to make this or any serious personal decision. It is not his personal and infallible calculation of the consequences of this decision, of the risks involved in this action that gives him security in his insecurity. It is his trust in the loving God who is calling that, in spite of his own proven weakness to date, makes it possible for him to achieve great things in his Christian living.

To have lost the sense of adventure in Christian living is to have lost an essential part of it. Perhaps this is the reason why Christianity has lost so much of its appeal to the young and venturesome. The stuffy and conservative terms in which the revolutionary message of Christ is frequently expressed, prevent them from understanding its real meaning. In it they find nothing to challenge them, nothing to hope for. It has all been achieved already.

For the depressed and weary the message of Christian hope must also be sounded clearly. Exhortations to hope

may not be used to support human injustice. Such 'pie in
the sky' quieting of the downtrodden is the very denial of
Christian hope, as it in the same breath approves the unchristian attitudes of those responsible, and ignores the
fundamental challenge of the Word-made-flesh. The search
for the divine must always be in and through the human.
The hope to which we summon them in the name of Christ
must always be accompanied by the loving care and service
of Christ.

For the sinner (and who is not?) the journey towards God
is also a journey back. The return cannot be accomplished
in one great stride. It demands, under the attracting power
of the divine love, time and patience. Man can move towards
God only one step at a time. His historical nature can only
express itself in time. We must not expect that we ourselves
or others will immediately attain to that freedom from sin
or from any particular proneness to sin which to some extent
will always be our lot. Grace and sin are not to be simply
opposed as two states which are mutually exclusive. There
is a really Catholic truth in the Lutheran expression, *simul
justus et peccator*, at once in grace and sinful. And it would be
better if as a substitute for the static image of state of grace
and of sin, we used that of the personal relationship as
outlined earlier with its degrees as well as its break-downs.
The development and decline of the relationship fits in well
the picture of the Christian life as a journey towards God
with its basic demand that one be facing in the right direction
and moving towards God rather than away from him. It is
this facing and moving towards him, however slowly, that is
the sign of one's acceptance of grace, of saying yes to the
divine invitation, of enjoying a personal relationship with
him, however undeveloped.

The penitent who genuinely repents of his sins and thus
turns in the right direction will not regard all individual
lapses which, despite his genuine seeking of God, occur in the
inevitable hangover from his previous condition, as dis-
rupting this basic relationship. He will realize that he can

only go forward from where he is and that the direction in which he is facing is more important than the speed at which he is travelling. So the sinner with some habitual failing which he is now determined with God's grace to break, should go forward in hope despite occasional recurrences of his failures. What has been acquired through time can only be finally removed with time, and the assurance of God's forgiving love and the hope which is ours in Christ must be always available to sustain the person along the road back.

No less in need of this personal hope is the scrupulous person. Some of these are in need of more than spiritual help. They are psychologically ill and need professional treatment by a psychiatrist. All of them need to be given hope. Very often they regard God as a hard taskmaster or all-seeing policeman who is trying to catch them out. (Where they may have got these ideas is another matter but parents and other educators should be very careful not to allow God to appear in this way.) They have no concept of God as loving and forgiving. They have only their own miserable experience to go on and so have no basis for hope in the future. A gradual recognition of God as he really is, will awaken this hope in the less serious cases and allow them to live a more normal, i.e., hopeful Christian life. For the others this must be combined with psychiatric help. (This is not meant as a full account of the pastoral handling of scrupulants.)

Without the comfort of hope there will be no step forward by miserable sinner or distressed scrupulant. Without the disturbance of hope there will be no advance by the comfortable or self-righteous. Without the challenge of hope Christianity can only appear to the young and idealistic as a prop of the *status quo*. To all these individuals hope comes as a divine gift, making possible a human response.

The Hope of the World

If Christ is human he is cosmic. The destiny which awaits man individually and in community cannot ignore the cosmos in which he becomes human and which becomes human in him. As man and the cosmos are bound up in their origins it is to be expected that their destinies will also be intertwined. St Paul's explicit testimony to this in his letter to the Romans (8:18 ff.) confirms the close relationship already amply evident in Scripture. Man is formed from the earth by God. God is the Lord of the cosmos also. To man as made in the divine image and so the climax of creation, the Lord of that creation entrusts it. In mastering the creation, humanizing it by harnessing its forces, man fulfils his God-given trust. He allows the glory of the Creator hidden in the cosmos to appear. He continues the work of creation.

The disharmony which man's sin introduced in his relations with God and his fellowman inevitably affected his relations with the cosmos as coming from God and destined for common development and enjoyment. The task of further creation was distorted by man's selfishness so that what should have been a bond between men became a constant source of division. What was intended for man's integrated growth served often to distract and divide him. What God meant as a reflection of himself and a way to him became instead a hindrance for man.

As the sin of man affected the world in this way so did the redemption first in promise and then in person counteraffect it. The reconciliation between God and man and that between man and man which is the fruit of that redemption also involves a reconciliation between man and the world. The final transformation which is the destiny of man and has already appeared in Christ is also intended for the world. In Christ the world, as well as man, has broken through to its final stage of development. It remains for Christ established in glory to extend this transformation to the human community and the world which has been entrusted to it. To achieve this he has given man a share not merely in creation but also in redemption, in transforming the cosmos through development, by harnessing it to the building of the one human community. With his eschatological vision the Christian is urgently summoned to enter into this activity of utilizing the resources of the world for the whole human community to which by divine right they belong. This is the response demanded in his cosmic situation. It is only by betraying this charge that he can opt out.

The technical development of the world forms a very important part of this task. As a means of organizing and releasing the natural energies of the world in the service of man technology is a humanizing force of unlimited value. However, where it is used, as it frequently is, for the exploitation or even destruction of some men rather than for the service of all, it becomes a dividing and dehumanizing force. Awareness of this ambiguity in technology as in all human achievement will not lead the Christian to despise or neglect it. He is no less committed to it because sinful men may and will abuse it; just as he does not reject Christ's adoption of material goods and sinful men as means of grace in the Church, although he is well aware of the abuses this may and does involve. What distinguishes his attitude is awareness of both these aspects of the world's goods; their capacity and indeed necessity for human development and their aptness for abuse by man tending to his own destruction. What sustains the Christian in this as in all else, is recognition of the final victory in Christ whereby the development of technology as of all the world's goods, is assured of ultimate value in the glorification of God and the service of man. What sustains him is hope.

It is not simply the spectacular achievements of technology that prepare the way for the eventual transformation of the world. All human work is of this kind. Therein lies its dignity. Work has been too often regarded as a punishment for sin. In some instances it was prescribed in a purely negative way as a means of mortification or as a way of keeping people 'off the streets'. It can have certain negative meanings of that kind but they are frustrating rather than developing for the Christian if they are not seen as the side-effects of the proper and positive value of work. It is in the context of developing the world's riches for personal and community use and enjoyment that all work, however menial and boring, has its meaning. To ensure the best results for the person and the community, care must be taken to see that as far as possible the person has the proper outlet for his talents, that they are devoted to serving the community in the best way in the circumstances and that the work itself is the most efficient use of material and time possible. Only in caring for all these does one show a correct regard for the Christian value of work as participating in the final transformation of the world through Christ. The development of automation for example is to be welcomed in this perspective as ensuring more effective processing of the world's goods for man's use and as releasing more people for more personal and creative kinds of work. (The problems of adjustment and the danger that such development will be used against former employees are very real. The obligation on all concerned to make sure this does not happen is equally real.)

In the second edition of his commentary on the letter to the Romans, Karl Barth says: 'If Christianity be not altogether and unreservedly eschatology, there remains in it no relationship whatever to Christ.' To say the least, the final transformation for which men and their world are destined in Christ, must pervade every Christian doctrine and practice. As a way of understanding and conducting human life, Christianity is directed towards the future.

It is this direction which has made possible the beginnings of a dialogue with the Marxists. They too are concerned with the future of mankind and with building a unified and just human society through using the resources of the cosmos. Within this general common orientation there are abyss-like differences, but at least these can now be explored for their true significance by committed thinkers from two of the most powerful and complete visions of man which the world has as yet experienced. The source of their attractive power lies undoubtedly in their capacity to generate hope. The ultimate victory of Christianity must rest on the fact that we have a more powerful hope, the hope which is Christ. But in so far as Marxists can implicitly share out hope and respect more and more the true nature of man founded like his hope in Jesus Christ, Christians will find means of collaborating with them and indeed of learning from them.

In this dialogue as in the perspectives opened up by Teilhard de Chardin the polarizing force of the *ta eschata* is seen to dominate human life and activity. Christian morality as the study of Christian living has to be developed with this orientation. For man, the person in community to whom the cosmos has been entrusted in order that he carry on the transforming work of Christ, his every good activity will, as fulfilling this trust, be a step forward into the unknown under the enabling and guiding power of Christ and his Spirit. It will be an expression of hope.